WITHDRAWN FROM
THE NEELB LIBRARY SERVICE
ON ....
FOR SALE AT £0.50

Long Stays in
BELGIUM AND LUXEMBOURG

Also available in this series from David & Charles:
LONG STAYS IN AMERICA
LONG STAYS IN AUSTRALIA

Coming Soon:
LONG STAYS IN FRANCE
LONG STAYS IN PORTUGAL

Long Stays in BELGIUM AND LUXEMBOURG

A COMPLETE, PRACTICAL GUIDE TO LIVING AND WORKING IN BELGIUM AND LUXEMBOURG

CAROLE HAZLEWOOD

DAVID & CHARLES
Newton Abbot   London

HIPPOCRENE BOOKS
New York

British Library Cataloguing in Publication Data
Hazlewood, Carole
  Long Stays in Belgium and Luxembourg: a
  complete, practical guide to living and
  working in Belgium and Luxembourg.
  1. Belgium—Handbooks, manuals, etc.
  2. Luxembourg—Handbooks, manuals,
  etc.
  I. Title
  914.930443   DH418
ISBN 0-7153-8837-1

First published in Great Britain by David & Charles 1987

© Carole Hazlewood 1987

All rights reserved. No part of this
publication may be reproduced, stored
in a retrieval system, or transmitted,
in any form or by any means, electronic,
mechanical, photocopying, recording or
otherwise, without the prior permission
of David & Charles Publishers plc

Typeset by Typesetters (Birmingham) Ltd
Smethwick, West Midlands
and printed in Great Britain
by A. Wheaton & Co Ltd, Hennock Road, Exeter
for David & Charles Publishers plc
Brunel House   Newton Abbot   Devon

Published in the United States of America
by Hippocrene Books Inc
171 Madison Avenue, New York, NY 10016
ISBN 0-87052-348-1 (United States of America)

Contents

1	Welcome to Belgium and Luxembourg	7
2	Things to Do Before Leaving	11
3	Being a Foreigner Abroad	20
4	Work and Business	32
5	Where to Live	52
6	Moving In	69
7	Education for All Ages	86
8	About Health and Health Services	101
9	Day-to-Day Living	108
10	Eating and Drinking, and Shopping	125
11	Travelling Around	140
12	Getting to Know the Country	153
13	Keeping in Touch with Home	169
14	To Stay On or to Leave	176
	Appendix 1: Relevant Addresses	180
	Appendix 2: Glossary	190
	Further Reading	193
	Acknowledgements	196
	Index	198

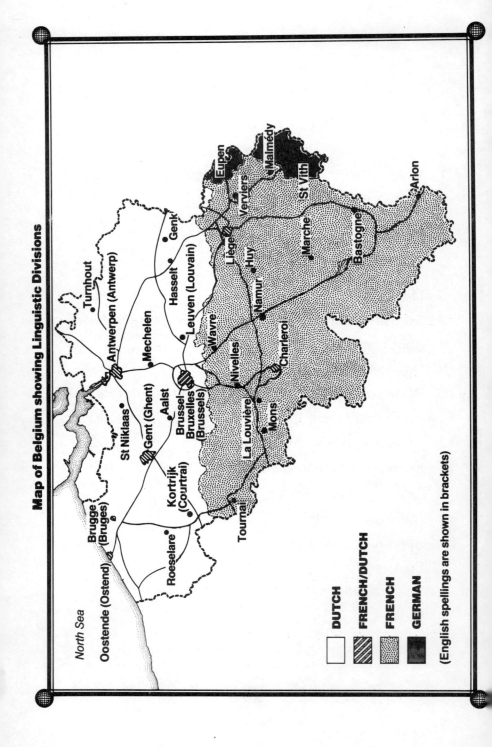

1
Welcome to Belgium and Luxembourg

Different people will have different reasons for a long stay, or for considering a long stay, in Belgium or Luxembourg: they may come to work; they may come to study; or they may come in order to be closer to people already living in these countries. Often, a post abroad can mean an enormous step forward in one's career. In any case, it will provide the opportunity of coming to grips with a foreign language which, in today's world, can prove a great advantage. Whatever the reason for your long stay, however, it is hoped that this book will make the transition from your present to your new home as easy as possible.

Moving house is always an ordeal; going to live abroad, for however short a stay, can be quite traumatic, particularly if you have no knowledge of what it is going to involve.

One thing I have noticed, too, over the years I have lived in Belgium, is that newcomers are usually so engrossed in finding somewhere to live that they first begin to make contact with those who can help them only when all the red tape has been dealt with. This book is aimed at filling such a gap and assisting in sailing through the seemingly unnecessary amount of paperwork.

It cannot be emphasised enough how important it is to tackle the paperwork in the right order. Unfortunately, there are no short cuts and you will find yourself wasting both time and patience if you do not follow the prescribed order. Also, in Belgium it is important to start off in the right language, since speaking French to a Fleming will not be appreciated nor will Flemish to a Walloon.

If you move to either of the two countries for longer than

Welcome to Belgium and Luxembourg

three months you will need to go through the formalities explained in Chapters 2 and 6. Strictly speaking, anyone staying in a private household for more than eight days and less than three months is required to report to the nearest local authority. However, this is not usually enforced for guests holidaying for a few weeks.

For a large number of English-speaking people moving to one of the two countries, usually brought by their work, it is the first time that they will live abroad. Anyone with a family will have to make the decision as to whether to uproot and come as a unit or whether the husband comes on his own and commutes at weekends where feasible. (A number of service people at SHAPE, with homes in southeast England, manage it.) Where the wife has a good job, she may be reluctant to give it up; for reasons which will become evident, it may not be possible or advisable for her to work in Belgium. Also, if children are settled in their schools or approaching some important examinations, it may not be a good idea to move them. If you want to make the most of the experience, it is essential that everyone enjoys it.

There are a great many single people, too, who move to one or other of the two countries; companies are generally happier about moving unmarried people or young couples where the problem of educating children does not arise.

I have tried to write this book bearing in mind, particularly, the business person moving abroad for the first time, the family with one or two children of school age, the single person and young couples; nevertheless, perhaps it will be of use to those who are old hands at moving around the world, as well as to the student who is following a course at one of the Belgian universities. Although an important part of the text has been given of necessity to settling into life in the two countries, I hope that the rest of the book will be of interest, too, to those who are really tourists but who want to know more than the normal guide book tells about what makes these countries tick.

In many things, Belgium and Luxembourg are closely linked; in fact, they are sometimes referred to jointly as the Belux. The present Grand Duchess of Luxembourg is sister to the King of the Belgians. Long before the creation of the Common Market, in 1921, Belgium and Luxem-

Welcome to Belgium and Luxembourg

bourg joined together in the Belgo-Luxembourg Economic Union. The value of the two currencies is the same, one Belgian franc (FB or BF, depending on which language you are speaking) being equal to one Luxembourg franc (Flux). A certain amount of recent legislation is the same in both countries and both have within their territory a part of the beautiful, deeply forested 'mountainous' region of the Ardennes (an extension of the Eifel).

Their links are so strong that it is natural to put the two countries together in one book. To avoid unnecessary repetition, I have written the book from the point of view of someone moving to Belgium since more expatriates move to that country than to Luxembourg. Where there are any variations for Luxembourg, these have been given at the end of the chapter.

Where the name and address of an authority in Brussels has been given, the first version is in French and followed by its Dutch equivalent since, depending on where you live, you will need to use the relevant local language. The glossary at the end of the book contains a list of useful words and terms you will need in the two languages.

In today's world where prices are continually going up it makes little sense to quote actual costs. Even if they move very little, one can never be sure what the exchange rate will do from one week to the next. Therefore, I have tried to indicate where prices are comparable or more expensive or less expensive than in Britain and the United States. At the moment of writing the exchange rate is about F65 to the pound sterling and F45 to the US dollar.

Inevitably, when moving anywhere, whether it is within your own country or whether it is abroad, there are hard decisions to be made and the period of resettlement to be overcome. However, if you do decide to move to Belgium or Luxembourg you will soon find that there are numerous advantages to be had. Both countries are very beautiful and between them they only possess one or two unattractive industrial towns. But they do have many well worth visiting: Brussels, Bruges, Antwerp, Liège and Luxembourg to name just a few. The countries are quaintly small: Belgium covers only 30,513sq km (11,780 sq miles); Luxembourg is even tinier with 2,586sq km (998sq miles). And the way of life is very comfortable.

Welcome to Belgium and Luxembourg

The people are hard-working, especially the Flemish who, in recent years, have built up their industry whilst that of Wallonia, sadly, has declined drastically. Foreigners, especially the British and the Americans, are made particularly welcome. In fact, they would never be referred to as foreigners by a Belgian. Britain has historical ties with Belgium which go back even before Queen Victoria's uncle was proclaimed the first King of the Belgians in 1831 and these have been cemented during this century by Britain's ready support in liberating the country in both world wars. Both Belgium and Luxembourg, too, still remember the part played by the United States in World War II.

Belgium, in particular, is steeped in culture. It contains many castles that are just as beautiful as the French châteaux of the Loire. You can explore the Flemish countryside at any time of the year and feel yourself living a Brueghel painting. Wallonia is rich in folklore and colourful traditions.

Another of Belgium's outstanding advantages is its cuisine. To a Belgian, eating is a pastime, a hobby — and one that is taken very seriously. In fact, there is a Belgian saying 'It is better to live to eat than eat to live'. Visit a few Belgian restaurants and you will soon discover why.

From a climatic point of view, the two countries experience weather similar to that of Britain, with the Belgian coastal regions having the same sort of climate as south-east England and Luxembourg's being more like that of the north of England. In other words, the farther south you travel the greater the differences in temperature: the coast, which is very sandy and ideal for sunbathing in summer, is generally mild, even in winter, but the Ardennes can be cold and have heavy snowfalls, making skiing very popular.

I am sure that you will enjoy your stay however long it is, and maybe you will be tempted to join the ranks of those who never move on.

2
Things to do Before Leaving

Your decision made to move to Belgium or Luxembourg, the next step is to plan your departure. Your preparations will fall into two parts: those pertaining to leaving your present home and work; and those pertaining to moving to your new country. Do allow yourself plenty of time to accomplish everything; officialdom anywhere in the world has its own peculiar pace for doing things. The amount of time you will need to be ready will depend very much on how complicated are your affairs and how many people are involved.

Property
What you decide to do with your property during your absence will be governed to a large extent by the length of time you are sure of staying abroad. Is there a chance that you will be returning to the same area earlier than planned? If there is, you will certainly not want to let property on a long-term basis. Whilst British law is supposed to restore people's property to them, where it is the only home they have, if they have let it during an absence abroad, it can take many months to effect in practice.

On the other hand, if you have been told that you are being sent to Belgium for three years, can you be 100 per cent sure that three years really will be only three years? It is certainly not unheard of for someone to be moved for a set time and to be still abroad at least ten years later.

If you rent an unfurnished house or flat in Britain on a normal three-, five- or seven-year lease, it should be stated in the contract that permission to sub-let cannot be withheld unreasonably by the landlord, provided it is done on a furnished basis and for a fixed term.

Those who own a house or a flat, or hold it on a long

Things to Do Before Leaving

lease (that is, ninety-nine years or less), will have to decide whether to let it during absence abroad or to leave it empty. If you decide to let it, then this should be under the terms of a furnished agreement and for a fixed term of not less than six months and no longer than one-year-less-one-day, even though your tenants contemplate staying longer. After 364 days, a new agreement can be negotiated, perhaps with an appropriate rent adjustment. On day 366, the property nominally returns to you so that you can reaffirm your sovereignty, even if you do not move back in.

Alternatively, you may rent the property on a short hold tenancy of up to five years and at a fixed 'fair rent' set by the local authority. This has not proved a popular arrangement although it might suit someone living in a remote area where the tenant would be virtually on his own.

During the term of a furnished letting, you will not have access to your home, except with the tenant's permission and accompanied by the agent, if one is involved. Nor can you terminate the agreement before it expires, except under extraordinary circumstances which are normally reserved for military and diplomatic personnel who will have a 'recovery clause' written into the contract.

No tenancy should be granted without a 'statutory notice' being served on the tenants prior to occupation; this recognises you as the owner/occupier of the property under the Rent Act (1977) or any subsequent enactment.

It is inadvisable to let your flat or house unfurnished for a short period. Not only may it be difficult to recover possession when you want to but the movement of furniture in and out causes more than fair wear and tear.

If you do decide to let property in Britain you can do so through a qualified solicitor, or you can use a property management agency. Should your property be mortgaged, you must inform your bank or building society of your intention to let so that formal consent can be given. It is recommended, too, that a copy of the agreement prepared by your solicitor or your agent is sent to the financing institution for its approval.

Once a tenancy has been agreed, the tenants will pay a deposit to the agents – usually a sum equivalent to a

Things to Do Before Leaving

calendar month's rent — and then it will be 'under offer' to them. This deposit is not the rent but a guarantee of the terms of the tenancy and for your fixtures, fittings and furniture; it is returned to the tenants on termination of the tenancy and provided the premises are left in good order and that there are no outstanding bills.

Of course, it is possible to handle the letting of your property in Britain yourself. Belgium is not that far away. However, you must be prepared to stay around until you find a suitable tenant and then to remain a day or two longer — the time it will take to check references, draw up and sign the lease, arrange the changeover with the necessary services, check the inventory together and hand over the keys. Needless to say, it will be much more difficult for anyone living in the United States to arrange for the renting of their own property.

If you decide to leave your property unoccupied for more than a few weeks, you should notify your insurance company which will make the necessary changes to your cover. It is also advisable to arrange for some security system. Your local police force can advise on suitable installations. In any case, it is best to notify them if the property is to remain unoccupied for any length of time and to let them know the name and address of anyone who will be taking care of it in your absence.

Animals
You may bring an animal into Belgium with a health certificate and proof of vaccination against rabies but the day you want to return to Britain for good you will be faced with either leaving it behind or putting it in quarantine. You will not be able to bring it with you on holiday to Britain, although holidays spent in most continental countries will mean that it can travel with you. America does not have such restrictions and pets, with the right shots, can travel freely between the States and Belgium and Luxembourg. Any specific questions relating to transporting a particular bird or animal between Britain and Belgium can be put to the Ministry of Agriculture, Fisheries and Food, Animal Health Division, Government Buildings, Hook Rise South, Tolworth, Surbiton, Surrey KT6 7NF.

Things to Do Before Leaving

Schooling
Parents with school-age children will have to decide whether or not to change their children's school and bring them to Belgium. The decision will probably depend on the age of the children, how long you are likely to live abroad, what possibilities exist for them to continue at their present school and what the plans are for their final education.

Parents of very young children generally want the family to stay together and the children can usually be placed in local schools for a few years. However, before they reach the age of eleven it will be necessary for them to be firmly integrated into the eventual education system you intend them to follow. Of course, if the school they are attending in the home country has a boarding element to it that may provide the ideal solution. Boarding-school education in Britain costs about as much as English-speaking day-school education in Belgium or Luxembourg.

If you are considering moving secondary school age children to Belgium with you and putting them into one of the English-speaking schools, it would be advisable to check first that the quality of the education in each child's main subjects is at least on a par with, if not better than, that being received at the present school.

If you decide to take your children with you – and it does provide an excellent opportunity for them to learn at least one foreign language and to mix with other nationalities – you should ask the present school head for a special report on the work and system that each of your children has been following. In addition, you should take all the latest reports and any other relevant document pertaining to each child's education for the new school to see.

Medical Attention
If you have a good doctor and dentist you will probably feel happier visiting them for a check-up before you leave the country. If you are being treated for a particular condition, a letter from your doctor or any relevant X-rays should be obtained to ensure that your new medical adviser can prescribe the correct medicines or treatment. It may also help to avoid unnecessary duplication of tests. Some physicians prefer not to hand such information to

Things to Do Before Leaving

patients and it may be that you will have to send the name and address of your new Belgian doctor, once these are known, to your previous one for records to be transferred.

Official Documents
If you hold a British passport which states that you are a British citizen, or if you hold an older one that states that you have the right of abode in Britain, you can obtain a Belgian identity card as a Common Market national without any difficulty on arrival in the country. If you hold a current British driving licence, you should take this with you to Belgium where it will be exchanged for a local one without your having to pass a further driving test. The only other official document that you should take with you when leaving the country is a copy of your birth certificate and that of every other member of the family accompanying you.

Anyone who does not hold a passport issued by a Common Market country or who holds a British passport with British Dependent Territories Citizenship or British Overseas Citizenship can only obtain an identity card in Belgium once a work permit has been issued. (In the case of a family, the other members automatically receive identity cards, too, the moment a work permit has been granted to the wage owner.) Work permits are obtained by employers and, at first, the permit is valid only for that specific employer.

The way the system is arranged, if you are not considered a national of a Common Market country, that is, if you do not qualify for a Belgian identity card as previously explained, you cannot move your home into the country before obtaining work. You are expected to have a job prior to establishing yourself in the country. Your employer should obtain your work permit, or the assurance that one will be granted to you, before you move to Belgium. In order to obtain your temporary residence permit — and in addition to a work permit — you will need a recent certificate of good conduct and morality relating to the past five years and testified to by a person over twenty-one years of age who is not related to you. This document must be witnessed by a Justice of the Peace or a Commissioner for Oaths and will have to be obtained

Things to Do Before Leaving

prior to leaving your present country of residence. (A model can be obtained from the Belgian Embassy.)

An American, and anyone else not qualifying through Common Market nationality for a Belgian identity card, must obtain a visa for himself and for each person accompanying him who does not meet the 'EEC' nationality requirement.

If you want to be self-employed and are not an EEC-national you will need a Professional Card. You should obtain the necessary forms, for yourself and for any member of your family accompanying you, from the visa section of the nearest Belgian embassy or consulate. Your application should be made for an Authorisation for Provisional Sojourn and a Professional Card, and be accompanied by the following: a written reference that you are a permanent resident in the country from which you are applying; eight passport-style photographs (four for the authorisation and four for the professional card); three copies of the form *Demande de Carte Professionnelle pour Etrangers*, obtained from the visa section and duly filled in; a medical certificate signed by a doctor on the list provided by the visa section; a recent certificate of good conduct and morality relating to the last five years; written banking and professional references; and visa applications for any other member of the family accompanying the applicant. There will be a charge for the documents, the amount of which will be indicated by the visa section when forwarding the necessary forms. This fee must be sent with the full application. It is important that no document is more than a few months old.

If you are a British citizen and contribute, or have contributed prior to retirement, to the National Health Service, you are entitled to medical treatment in any of the EEC countries on the same terms as the people of the country to which you are moving. In order to receive the benefit of this EEC agreement, you should contact the Overseas Branch of the Department of Health and Social Security, Newcastle-upon-Tyne, NE98 1YX (Tel 0632 857111) to obtain the form E111 before leaving the United Kingdom. This applies, too, to people visiting the country.

Things to Do Before Leaving

Removing
Before you decide to move all your personal belongings with you, it would be wise to pay a visit to your new country to select your new home. In that way you will not ship too much or too little furniture. Also, the law requires that you provide proof of a place of residence in the new country before moving your belongings.

When choosing a removal company, check the type of insurance coverage each holds and the cost and coverage of any additional policy proposed. These vary greatly from company to company. When valuing your belongings for insurance coverage, be sure to declare the new replacement price in your country of destination. A piece of Waterford crystal will cost far more to replace in Belgium than in Ireland.

It is better to let the movers pack everything so that if there is any damage you can make a claim. The packer will make an inventory of all you are having moved, in the correct language, which you will have to sign. A copy of this will be given to you and this is your receipt from the removal company for your goods. You can import free of duty into Belgium any personal effects, such as furniture, linen, silver, canned foodstuffs where these are for personal consumption, household items, clothing, motor cars (which should be mentioned on the inventory even though you are driving them over), motor cycles, bicycles and tools or equipment, provided that you have owned them and used them for six months. Items imported as personal effects cannot be sold within twelve months of the date they enter the country. Anything that forms part of the stock of a trade or profession, such as foodstuff, liquor and items for resale by a business, are not exempt from duty. Any new goods you choose to import will be subject to Belgian VAT (TVA/BTW) and import duties (from the US) at the relevant rate. Special licences are required to import wines, spirits and weapons and can be obtained from Office Central des Contingents et Licences, Rue de Mot 24-26, 1040 Brussels.

If you are including British-made light fittings with your personal effects, be sure to add a good supply of light bulbs as Belgian light sockets use the screw-in type of bulb. Most other British household appliances, after

LSLB-B

Things to Do Before Leaving

changing the plugs to the standard continental two round-pin variety, will be usable in Belgium where the voltage is almost completely 220 volts, 50 cycles per minute nowadays. Very occasionally you can still find 110 volts but this is now rare. However, American electrical equipment will usually require a transformer (which can be purchased in Belgium) but cannot help for items using 60 cycles.

Money
You will probably want to arrange for some money to be deposited for you in a Belgian bank account so that you are able to cover initial expenses. Since this is likely to become your current account, it is best to transfer the money to your British bank's Belgian corresponding bank as British banks in Belgium are really there to handle company business and not private accounts. You will need to allow about ten days to two weeks for the money to arrive and the Belgian bank will want to see your passport or identity card to justify your opening an account or withdrawing the money.

Wills
Now that you are leaving your homeland, it may be a good time to put your affairs in order and to make a will, if you have not done so already. As long as Britain is regarded as your country of residence a will made there will relate to any property, possessions or money you have in that country.

Travel
If you are planning to move some or all of your possessions yourself from Britain you would be advised to arrange to travel direct to Belgium as any journey taking you through France or Holland will involve complicated documentation as your belongings should pass through these countries in transit. However, if you are making the journey with just a few clothes to tide you over until the main part of your luggage arrives, then there should be no difficulty over you arriving via one of the other neighbouring countries which may prove the quicker journey.

Things to Do Before Leaving

Temporary Accommodation
It is possible that your future employer will organise temporary accommodation for you. If this is left to you to arrange, contact the nearest Belgian Tourist Office for the official hotel guide. In Brussels and Antwerp there are special 'aparthotels' where you can rent small flats at a better rate than in the bigger hotels. These are ideal if you expect to be there for a few weeks since they have small kitchens that allow you to cook for yourself.

To double check that you have forgotten nothing and that there have been no major changes in the law since this book was written, contact the nearest Belgian Embassy or Consulate to obtain the documentation they provide for people moving to Belgium. And, whether or not you ask for the hotel guide, contact the tourist office to find out what you can about your new homeland before you arrive.

Specifically About Luxembourg
Schooling
Parents going to live in Luxembourg with children of secondary school age will find the choice of school extremely limited (see Chapter 7).

Official Documents
The requirements for EEC nationals entering Luxembourg to live are the same as those for Belgium. However, the names by which certain documents for non-EEC nationals are known do vary slightly. The visa to gain entry is called an *Autorisation de Séjour Provisoire*. In order to obtain this, five copies of the application form must be filled in and submitted with three recent passport-type photographs and the *Déclaration Patronale*, which is the contract issued by the employer and stamped by the state.

3
Being a Foreigner Abroad

Wherever you live in the world away from your homeland, be it Belgium or Peru, you will find certain things that are done in a different way: different customs, different laws, different traditions, and different ethics. If you are not to feel like an outsider, you have at least to acknowledge these differences, even if you feel unable to embrace all of them. Where they are the laws of the country, of course, you are bound to accept them. Such experiences add enormously to the great adventure that living in another country, among another nation, presents.

Whether it is to Belgium or even to some English-speaking country that you have decided to move, the initial settling in period is never easy. 'Culture shock' affects different people in different ways: it can vary from a simple homesickness that you would experience when moving to another part of your own country, to a very pronounced difficulty in accepting the local way of life. Much is caused by the long working hours that are often expected by foreign companies. Although there are legal limits set and overtime is not officially allowed at the present moment, most people with a good, interesting job who want to keep it will work as long as is necessary. And, since expatriates are invariably paid better salaries and have more tax advantages than the Belgians, it is a question of weighing up the advantages and the disadvantages. However, families do tend to suffer when father spends long days and, even perhaps, weekends at work, and then, even longer periods travelling abroad.

The foreign communities are very aware of the problem since most expatriates have been through culture shock to some degree. The local clergy and ministers are used to helping with such situations, and the communities in Belgium have set up an organisation to help those in need: the Community Help Service. It has a marvellous 'help-line' 24-hour telephone service which not only operates to provide comfort and advice to those who are finding it difficult to cope with life's problems but which will give the answers to a mass of practical questions.

Moving to Belgium or Luxembourg need be very little different from moving to the farthest extreme of your own country. Most Belgians are pro the British, despite the catastrophe of May 1985's Heysel football match and previous less-deadly − although not dissimilar − incidents, which have been just as degrading for the country's British population. Although we have now known more than forty years of peace in western Europe, the Belgians cannot forget the way the British fought to attain freedom for them in the '1914–18' and the '1940–44' wars, as they are generally known here. The Americans are equally welcome, too, and have played an important part in the Belgian economy. American business has invested more in Belgium than any other nation and a good deal of technical know-how has also been imparted.

One of the greatest difficulties all foreigners encounter in living in Belgium is knowing when to use which language with the not quite ten million population. Because there are three national languages − French, Dutch and German − it does not mean that you can choose to speak whichever one you want. You have to know when to use each one. If you should use the wrong one you can find yourself with serious problems and, in business, such a *faux pas* can cost you a good relationship, even a transaction.

If there are any rules to go by, the first is to know what part of the country you are in linguistically and, accordingly, to speak the language of that region. For that you will need to learn the map of Belgium and to study the linguistic 'frontier' which cuts the country in two from near Mouscron in the west to close to Visé in the east. (See map on page 6.) Everything north of that line, with the exception of Brussels, is in Flemish territory; that is, the official language is Dutch, Flemish being a dialect of Dutch. To the south lies the French-speaking part of the country. German is spoken in the regions to the extreme east, close to the German border.

Being a Foreigner Abroad

Never make the mistake of trying to speak French in the Flemish part of the country. If you do not know sufficient Dutch to open a conversation, speak in English. Having established that you are not a Belgian, any Fleming more at ease in French than in English will ask you if you speak French. You can then continue in that language. People not used to mixing with foreigners do not always hear an English accent and you will be immediately classified as an impolite Walloon (inhabitant from the south of the country) if you start off in French. Also, they are pleased that foreigners are aware at least that French is not the only official language.

If you meet somebody socially and have not been formally introduced, it would be wisest to speak in English unless you are sure that French is his mother tongue. Names are no indication either, since there has been much intermarriage over the years, and the most Flemish-sounding name can belong to a person of French mother tongue and a French-sounding name can easily belong to a Fleming.

The Flemings' intolerance of being addressed in French is quite understandable when you come to appreciate the country's background. For centuries the language of the various royal and religious courts situated on the land, now known as Belgium, had been French, despite the fact that the language of the people in the northern part of the country (then the Low Countries) was Flemish. The Flemings were the underdogs, mostly illiterate, and occupied in the most menial employment. If they wanted to improve their lot they had to learn French. Today, more than 60 per cent of the Belgian population is Flemish, of which a large part speaks French as well. By comparison, few Walloons have ever tried to master the Dutch language and, consequently, they find themselves in an inferior position when looking for good jobs. The Flemings, on the other hand, with Dutch as a mother-tongue (not one of the most important languages in world affairs) have had to learn other languages to survive.

The German region is much more tolerant but you may not always find someone who speaks French.

Brussels is officially bilingual, although French is spoken by the majority of the inhabitants. It also has its own dialect, known as *Bruxellois*, which is a colourful mixture of both languages. In Brussels, when dealing with civil servants, if you are able to speak Dutch you will soon find out that invariably it makes life easier to use that language. Of course, in certain ministries that have been established specifically for one part of the country, such as for French Culture and for Dutch Culture, then you would be expected to speak the respective language.

The Belgians are surprisingly tolerant of much else. As long as you do not interfere with them and their way of life you will be free to do more or less what you want in their country. The 'live and let live' attitude has its roots in the centuries of occupation when, to survive, the people had to tolerate their occupiers.

Regular occupation has also produced a certain lack of discipline. The Belgians are very reluctant to queue anywhere and, until recently, this was regularly enforced in public offices by a number system. Wherever you went, on entering you tore the next number off a block of tickets and waited for it to be called. This has largely gone out of fashion, although it can still be found in certain government departments and has been adopted in some places in the private sector, such as at the delicatessen counter of some supermarkets.

Their less-pleasing characteristic — aggressiveness — probably has the same origins. You will notice it especially behind the driving wheels of their cars if, woe and betide you, you dare to take their priority! As individuals they are no more aggressive than the British.

Discipline on the roads has been taught by the introduction of driving licences, reducing the number of roads having priority and setting heavy fines for speeding and for serious offences. Twenty years ago virtually every road entering another from the right had priority, even those entering a major road. (Nowadays, priority is always indicated in cases where it is not given to the road coming from the right.) Whilst the standard of driving has improved enormously over the last twenty years, and the Belgians are much better at giving signals and better motorway drivers than the British, it is inadvisable to take someone's priority. If you intend to drive in Belgium, you must learn the local highway code quickly. (Some of the more important driving rules are given in Chapter 11).

You will find that it is not usual to arrive on time in Belgium, except for doctors' and dentists' appointments. People generally arrive a good fifteen minutes late, politely termed the 'academic quarter of an hour' after the length of time academics took to greet each other prior to starting a meeting or lecture – and it can be even longer. No public performance starts on time and the traditional 'banging on the boards' still heralds the opening of a play.

Belgians are on the whole very conservative. They dress well and know good quality when they see it. In the service industries, you may find the younger and artistic members of the staff dressing casually but in most other businesses office workers will be dressed traditionally. Modern, trendy styles are generally for the young; anyone over thirty tends to wear classic styles.

In other things, too, the taste is generally conservative and sometimes a good many years behind the fads in America and Britain. The Britain pub went through a period of great popularity here a few years ago, although the style had to be much adapted to Belgian habits. New ideas, too, tend to arrive and catch on about ten years after they have been adopted in Britain: garden centres, for instance, have started to spring up in the last one or two years. Greetings cards, too, have only just started to catch on. Undoubtedly the language problems of the country contribute considerably to this delay in progress in that every piece of printed matter (from packaging to order forms and literature) has to be produced in at least two languages which greatly increases the initial outlay.

Christian names are not used easily. You will be addressed as Monsieur, Madame or Mademoiselle by a *francophone* (the local term for a French speaker), or as Mijn Heer, Mevrouw or Juffrouw by a Fleming, far longer than in Britain or America, unless the people you meet mix regularly in international circles. And a single woman from her mid-thirties on will be addressed as Madame by anyone who does not know her well. It is normal, too, to shake hands on meeting people and on leaving them. Even young children will expect you to shake their hand.

The lifestyle is more conservative, too, than in Britain. Most young people live at home until they get married. It is quite unusual to hear of a young person leaving home to live alone, and even rarer to hear of girls or boys sharing an apartment. Some students studying away from home may have a small pied-à-terre and live near their seat of learning during the week, invariably returning to the parental home at weekends.

The family is extremely important and it is not unusual for the different members to come together every weekend. Young people tend to have more friends than their elders but family and family life have to take precedence.

You will probably not make many Belgian friends while you are here and it will take you a long time to be invited into a Belgian home. If you are invited it will probably be to eat in a restaurant first before you are asked to their house. In return, you should invite your hosts to your home and it is good etiquette to write a thank-you note.

When you visit a Belgian home you should take a small gift: flowers, or one of the attractive plant arrangements on sale here, are perhaps the safest choice as they are appreciated by most people. However, never offer those large chrysanthemums, particularly the white variety that come into the shops at the end of October, for these are taken in great quantities to the cemeteries on 1 November, All Saints' Day.

Chocolates, especially the handmade, cream-filled *pralines*, are generally very welcome, too, as gifts for your hosts. The best makes are considered to be Godiva, Corné de la Toison d'Or, Neuhaus, and Wittamer (which also makes fabulous pastries and cakes). Avoid the cheaper, industrially made chocolates, such as Léonidas. Quality is far more important to a Belgian than quantity.

If you are invited to a Belgian home, it is not usual to offer a bottle of wine or alcohol, unless you have visited there many times before. Where there are children in the family, some small gift for them will be appreciated by the parents, too.

Eating is one of the Belgians' favourite pastimes and their cuisine is one of the best in the world. It is rare to eat badly and even a Frenchman, being honest, will admit that, taken generally, the Belgian cuisine is better than his own.

At the table, it is rare to find bread plates and knives set.

Until recently, you would only find such sophistications in the best of restaurants but, with the adoption of *nouvelle cuisine*, some of the middle-priced establishments are acquiring the habit. When there is no plate you simply place your roll or slice of bread on the tablecloth, to the left of your knife and fork, and break it up there. For the butter, you use your main-course knife. Sometimes the required cutlery will be brought separately with each course.

Snails require their own implements: the tiny fork for hooking them out of their shells, and the special tongs with which to hold them. Lobsters, too, will be served with the special pick but crackers are not normally supplied, that part of the work having been done beforehand. Soup spoons are round and resemble the British dessert spoon. They are ideal for the thick tasty vegetable soups of which the Belgians are so fond.

It is usual to eat at least three courses for your meal, even at lunchtime. When dining out for pleasure, as opposed to eating during the working day, it is customary to order a starter. Since the majority of Belgian meals are cooked fresh, you will have to wait for your main course in any case and so you might as well spend the time sampling some small specialty which has been designed as an appetiser, to amuse the palate during that waiting period.

You will probably be disappointed at the lack of vegetables in most ordinary restaurants. Unless a specific vegetable is essential to a dish, such as the spinach in *oeufs pochés à la florentine*, you will probably receive only potatoes in at least 60 per cent of all restaurants. Chips (French fries) are not only the diet of the British; the Belgians are renowned *frite* eaters and generally cook them better than any other nationality. Steaks and steak tartare (*filet américain*) are invariably served with salad and chips.

Take care when using the condiments. Salt is usually placed in a multi-holed top similar to our pepper pot, and pepper in the single-holed top, which looks like our salt cellar.

The dessert is usually eaten after the cheese course and forks are not always provided. However, it is normal to receive a knife and fork for the cheese. Biscuits are rarely available for eating with cheese; bread, generally French, is provided if anything is required.

It is normal to drink wine or beer with your meal. Wine will be served even before the first course arrives as it is expected to accompany the whole meal, unlike in many British restaurants where you are expected to drink it only with the main course. Belgians will select different wines for different courses, depending on how well each wine marries with the respective dishes. However, it is becoming increasingly acceptable to drink red wine with fish. It is not usual to drink coffee or milk with a meal, except if you have ordered only a snack. Coffee, decaffeinated coffee, tea or a herbal tea (known as an infusion) can be ordered at the end of the meal and, if you ask for milk, they will all be accompanied by 'coffee milk', a sweet long-life version.

The Belgian's admirable quality of 'live and let live' shows no better than in a restaurant where eating, after all, is a hobby sacred to every Belgian. And yet, in eating houses not frequented by many foreigners, I have seen a glass of milk served with an *haute cuisine* meal and doggy bags provided – on request – and without the bat of an eyelid.

Belgians are very adventuresome in their cuisine and, on the whole, like tasting new dishes, so do not be afraid to serve one of your favourite recipes if you have guests at home. However, do not serve pork to Belgian guests on their first visit or for a major dinner party. As the cheapest meat – and not nearly so good as the pork we eat in Britain – it is only considered correct to serve at such times if it is in the form of a suckling pig.

One problem foreigners usually have in another country is knowing how much to tip and when. Tipping was much more frequent twenty years ago when, at times, it verged on being a bribe. Today, tips are included in taxi fares, in restaurant and café bills and the cost of having your hair done. There is certainly no need to give extra when taking a taxi (they are expensive enough) and it is less and less usual to leave anything as a tip in a restaurant. If you find the service especially good, then you could leave BF100 or BF200, but you are under no obligation. You should never leave a tip, however, when you are served by the owner. The same advice about restaurant tipping goes for a visit to the hairdresser's, too; in which case you would probably give BF40 or BF50 to a member of the staff who has served you. Some people leave tips and some people consider that the legal amount added to the bill as a tip is sufficient. But remember, once you start tipping it is difficult to stop.

There are other places or times, however, when you should tip. When you leave your coat, even in a restaurant, you are expected to tip the person who hands it back to you (unless it is the owner). In the case of some concert halls or theatres, it may be that you are asked for the tip, which is really the charge for cloaking your belongings, when you deposit them. There may be a fixed minimum for this. You can ask how much is required and you will either be told an amount per piece or 'whatever you want'. When you are shown to your seat at the cinema or, alternatively, when you have your ticket checked and the seat indicated to you, you must give a tip. Everyone else in the theatre — as well as you — will soon know if you have not or if what you gave was insufficient! In fact, in Belgium, usherettes receive only this payment for the work they do. It is usually the same for the 'toilet ladies' who demand money from men and women alike.

New Year is the one time of the year when you may be called on for a tip from people providing you with services. Your cleaning woman will certainly expect something, and, if you live in an apartment building, so will your concièrge, even if you are contributing to his wages through the charges billed in addition. Depending on what sort of an area you live in, other people may make their desires known, too; for example, the postman and the dustmen.

Just as eating is a delight in Belgium, so is shopping. The windows are dressed so temptingly and with such good taste and, generally, the quality is very high. It is relatively easy and fun to look for gifts to take or send home and you will find an interesting variety of things Belgian, certainly enough to cater for all tastes.

If you are here in July and August you will certainly be struck by the number of shops and restaurants (yes, even in the tourist area around Brussels' Grand Place) that close for their annual holiday. On the whole, most establishments close for a month but then they often work a full six- or seven-day week for the rest of the year. Nowadays, it is usual for various types of shop within one area to stagger their vacations, but before this all the bakers or all the laundries in one area would close together.

Another phenomenon of the holiday season is the way everybody rushes either to the coast or to the Ardennes. The resultant traffic jams and parking problems are enormous and, should you be heading for a cross-Channel ferry, can cause you serious delays. This habit is not just reserved for the traditional holiday months of July and August, but it takes place on every fine weekend from Easter through to October.

When they celebrate the Belgians certainly know how to do it in style and this can usually be appreciated on important occasions in their lives: a baptism, a 'solemn communion' which is similar to the Anglican confirmation, and a marriage. Funerals are generally impressive. Baptisms are invariably family occasions but, at the birth of the child, the parents will often offer sugared almonds to those attending the celebrations, to those who have offered gifts and to close friends and associates. In Belgium, traditionally pink is for a boy and blue for a girl, although this is changing.

The solemn communion is an important event which takes place when the child is about eleven or twelve years old. If you attend such an occasion, you will probably be invited to the church service and then on to the home or a restaurant for drinks, a luncheon consisting of many courses, and, perhaps, eventually supper.

Assisting at a Belgian wedding is quite an experience. In the country, the celebrations can go on all day and into the night. Often, there will be two ceremonies: the religious one and the civil one, which is the legal act of marriage. They will sometimes be held on different days with the religious ceremony always following the civil one. If there are two ceremonies, the celebrations will be held after the religious service. There is usually a big reception for friends and acquaintances of the couple before the family lunch or dinner, depending on what time the wedding takes place.

Many traditions are the same as we have in Britain: wedding lists are placed with shops; the bride will probably wear a smart suit for the civil ceremony but a long white dress for the church one; the groom generally wears grey morning dress of top hat and tails, or uniform if he is in one of the services; and the bride is often attended by a number of young children. But there are some differences. For instance, you can take your present with you to the celebrations or you can have it delivered beforehand and it is quite usual for people to offer bouquets of flowers to the bride. For the civil ceremony, the groom collects the bride and takes her to present her to their guests before they all leave for the town hall. He has with him the bride's bouquet which he chooses and offers to her. The partners usually exchange plain gold wedding rings, engraved inside with both their names and the date of the wedding, which they wear on the third finger of either the right or left hand, depending on preference.

Weddings, as with solemn communions, are often celebrated in a local restaurant or a large property rented for the occasion. It is not common to use a hotel. If these events are held at home, the catering is usually done outside.

When a member of the family dies at home, it is usual for the body to remain in the house until the funeral, unless, of course, for reasons of hygiene the body has to be moved to a mortuary. However, there are some communes where the body is moved to the local undertaker's mortuary; this is practised in Overijse, Tervuren and Zaventem close to Brussels, and in the region of Liège.

Death notices are usually printed and either sent through the post or delivered. In the country, you will probably receive death notices of anyone dying in your neighbourhood.

Hearses do not usually carry any mourners, being reserved for the undertakers, the coffin and the enormous floral tributes. Some hearses are quite elaborate with torch-like lights at each corner and black plumes. Close relatives and friends will go to the house or the undertakers, if that is where the body is resting, and will follow the hearse on foot to the church. After the ceremony, and before the coffin is taken to the cemetery or crematorium, it is usual for the close relatives of the deceased to greet those attending the ceremony and a plate is placed at the back of the church on which to leave your visiting card as a sign of your presence and confirmation of your condolences. A few words can be written on the reverse side if you wish.

It is usual to attend the funeral of a close member of the family of a colleague with whom one works, such as one of his parents, spouse or child. In cases where many members of the staff are concerned, companies sometimes delegate one or two members to represent them as a whole. Often a director will attend the funeral of a close relative of an employee who has worked a long time for the company. Friends will attend the funerals of close members of their friends' families, even though they may never have met the deceased. Your presence is considered a sign of esteem for your colleague or friend.

Specifically About Luxembourg
A great deal of what has been written concerns Luxembourg, too. However, its language problem is much simpler in that its 365,000 population speaks and writes several languages at the same time and throughout the whole country. You will find that street names, travel tickets, hotel registers and menus are in French; Luxembourg newspapers are written in German although a number of articles, mainly cultural, and a good many advertisements, as well as social announcements, appear in French. German is the main language in the churches. In everyday conversation, the Luxembourg dialect, with its limited vocabulary, is generally used with the discussion going into French or German when insufficiencies occur. French is used as much as possible but German is generally necessary when talking to people with less education.

In German you will be addressed as Herr, Frau or Fraulein instead of the French Monsieur, Madame or Mademoiselle.

4
Work and Business

Belgium and Luxembourg are not countries that naturally attract people to embark upon some spontaneous adventure into the unknown in the way that the sun draws people to the south of France and Italy. What is more likely to lead you to one of these countries, especially Belgium, is that it is at the hub of the Common Market. This is where you will meet an incredible number of different nationalities, where you can feel easily content in a country which puts less importance on social class than Britain, and where beautiful and varied scenery and a comfortable way of life are thrown in for good measure.

Employment
In addition to your professional skills, you will find it a distinct advantage, and in many cases essential, to be fluent in, or at least conversant with, one of the main national languages and to be able to understand a certain amount in the other. Gone are the days when international companies had British or American managing directors who insisted that everyone speak English with them. These positions have been largely filled by Belgians, and English alone is no longer sufficient. If your work is likely to involve negotiating with Belgian businesses or public authorities, you will find it essential to be able to understand their asides during a meeting.

Most people who move to the Belux do so because their companies transfer them there. Unless you find employment through an advertisement in a British or American newspaper, it is probably more practical to visit one of the countries for a few days to look for work. However, a special service has been set up within the Common Market countries to assist EEC nationals who are looking for employment in another member state and the British organisation is at the Manpower Services Commission.

Job advertisements are often placed in English in Belgian newspapers and the most important issue of the week for these is the Saturday-Sunday paper which comes out on Saturday morning. (Most major Belgian newspapers are first published in the evening with the next morning's editions updating the news.) There are no truly national Belgian papers in the sense that they cover the whole country's news and, for this reason, you would be well advised to look in at least one Flemish paper as well as a French-language one: *De Standaard* and *Het Laatste Nieuws* would be obvious recommendations for the Flemish press; and *Le Soir* for the French language. The local English weekly magazine, *The Bulletin*, also carries some job advertisements, although these are more likely to be of a clerical than managerial nature. *The Bulletin* can be obtained by subscription only, and for a minimum of six months.

Another way of finding work is to advertise yourself in one of the publications mentioned for the type of job you would like or to write to specific companies. It is possible to purchase copies of the *Year Book* of the British Chamber of Commerce for Belgium and Luxembourg, which contains the names and addresses of its members, and the American Chamber of Commerce in Belgium's annual *AmCham Directory*, which not only gives a list of its members but also contains details of all American companies in Belgium.

If you are looking for an executive position, there are a number of executive search agencies established in Belgium. You will find many are members of one or even both of the chambers of commerce mentioned and, therefore, are listed in the directories recommended above. You can send a written, detailed curriculum vitae and, if the search agency has an interest in your background, it will contact you. The search agency fee is paid by the client company and not the individual.

For those whose skills lie in the secretarial field, there are agencies to help them find work. Again, these companies are often members of one or both of the two chambers of commerce mentioned; they also advertise on a fairly regular basis in *The Bulletin*. They, too, do not

Work and Business

charge a fee to the person looking for work; it is the future employer who pays the agency. Most agencies will expect you to take tests relevant to the type of work you are seeking. However, if you are not an EEC national, the chances of obtaining a work permit for a secretarial job are very slender.

Anyone not needing a work permit and whilst looking for a permanent job could 'temp' for one of the many good temping (*interim*) agencies which hire out staff for a wide variety of work — in fact, anything from receptionist to telex operator and secretary to computer operator. No work permits are granted for temporary employees.

The regulations on employing anybody other than Common Market nationals are becoming tighter and tighter and you should not consider a position offered as firm until your work permit has been obtained. Belgium, like so many other countries today, has a serious unemployment problem; it is also experiencing a braindrain. By severely restricting the number of non-Common Market nationals entitled to work here, it is hoped to make more jobs available to Belgians and to encourage the most highly qualified sector of its labour force to remain within the country. Therefore, your prospective employer has to prove to the authorities that the job he is offering you cannot be done by a Belgian national.

First-time work permits (class 'B'), valid for one year, are not transferable and, if the holder wishes to change employment, the new employer must enter a fresh application. There are three categories in all. Domestic personnel receive 'C' permits, also valid for one year. All other employees receive a 'B' permit on arrival in the country that can be renewed for up to four years, when it is changed for a class 'A', which is of unlimited duration and valid for any employer.

There are certain professions — musicians, priests and ministers, full-time newspaper foreign correspondents, and directors of subsidiaries in Belgium, for example — that are exempt from the work permit requirement. If you have reason to think that it may not be required of you, contact your nearest Belgian embassy or consulate for confirmation.

It is usual to receive a contract from your employer

which you will be expected to sign prior to, or on the first day of employment. You should read it very carefully beforehand and, if in any doubt, take it to a lawyer. The contract will usually stipulate working conditions, such as hours and place, the job description and title, the amount of notice to be given by both sides in the event of its termination, the remuneration you are to receive and, perhaps, any additional advantages. However, the latter may form part of a separate agreement between the employer and you. Belgian law is extremely protective of all employees and can override any contract you may be asked to sign that does not conform with relevant legislation.

The working week today consists of 38½ hours. For nearly ten years (since Belgium first started to feel the economic recession) it has been illegal to remunerate any overtime worked. Employers are expected to repay additional hours with time off. Many sectors would like to see this law rescinded as it is detrimental to the productivity of the work force.

Salaries are generally high for Europe, but then, so are taxes. Multinational companies usually pay better than Belgian ones. If you are one of the lucky few who can take advantage of special fiscal concessions granted to certain executives, or if you work for the Common Market and pay only a token amount of income tax, you will live in relative luxury. However, there is no reason why other employees should not enjoy a comfortable life style, too. Read newspaper advertisements for comparable jobs and talk to specialists in the employment field to find out how much to ask for at an interview.

Another result of the economic crisis has been that salaries and wages have been tied to the retail price index for all employees. This means that there can be no merit rises, only promotion, and the whole workforce receives the same percentage increase at the same time. In addition to the regular salary, all employees having worked a full year are entitled to 'holiday money' equivalent to 85 per cent of the month's salary in which the vacation is taken. Most companies give employees an end-of-year achievement bonus or pay a 'thirteenth month'. These additional payments are very nice to have but are

Business

⁾ a higher rate of income tax than your regular

negotiating a salary in Belgium you should
⸱r the net amount that you will receive, not the
gross. Personal income taxes are high and social security charges are unlimited. It is normal for the net amount of your salary to be paid direct into your bank account, with all the deductions, such as income tax and social security, having been made by your employer and paid on your behalf. You will receive a monthly printed statement detailing the various payments.

The additional advantages you will be offered vary from company to company and will also depend on the type of employment offered. Executives of some companies, especially foreign or multinational ones, may be offered a company car, housing allowance, sports club membership or sports club facilities, schooling allowances and language courses. When an employee is transferred it is usual for his moving expenses and his eventual repatriation costs to be paid. Belgian companies do not normally offer many additional advantages to their staff; the costs of travelling to work, however, for those living outside the area are generally met by the company, and some organisations provide subsidised lunches. By law, companies employing more than three people must provide a dining-room where employees can eat their lunch.

Everyone is entitled to the ten public holidays per year as paid holidays; if it is necessary for you to work on one of those days or on a Sunday, you are entitled to take another day off. The public holidays are: New Year's Day (1 January), Easter Monday, Labour Day (1 May), Ascension Day, Whit Monday, Belgian National Day (21 July), the Feast of the Assumption (15 August), All Saints' Day (1 November), Armistice Day (11 November) and Christmas Day (25 December). In addition, the Flemings celebrate 11 July, Golden Spurs' Day, and the Walloons 24 September; most businesses in those regions close on their respective community day. In Brussels, a day off is normally arranged by mutual agreement between employer and employee. There are two more days when administrative offices and public authorities, schools and other such institutions close: the King's Name Day or the Day of the

Work and Business

Dynasty (15 November) and the second day of Christmas, the day we call Boxing Day in Britain (26 December).

After you have worked one calendar year, known as a reference year, you become entitled to four weeks' paid holiday in the following year. If you have not yet completed your reference year but want to take some holiday, and your employer agrees, you are entitled to two days off, with pay, for every complete month you have worked.

There are other occasions, too, when you may take time off without having the time deducted from your earnings. If you get married, the time allowed is either two or three days, depending on the type of work of the individual. In the case of a birth, the mother is entitled to fourteen weeks' paid leave, of which the first month is met by the employer and the rest by the mutuality; up to six weeks of this time can be taken prior to the birth. Should the mother work during those six weeks prior to the birth, an equal amount of time off can be added to the eight weeks taken after the child is born. The husband is allowed two days off for the birth of a child. The death of an immediate relative – a parent or a child living in the same house – entitles the bereaved to three days off; two days are granted for grandparents living in the same house and one day for grandparents living in another house. A day off is also accorded to parents for their child's solemn communion or the secular equivalent if they do not embrace the Roman Catholic religion. For those who decide to divorce their partner, the employer is obliged to give a day off but it will not be paid.

Many companies start the day early and it is not unusual for working hours to begin at 8am. Because a large number of employees live in the provinces and commute daily by road or train into Brussels, many companies have adopted flexitime. It is common for management to start work at the same time as the staff – and even earlier.

If you are working in an international office environment you will find that relationships are generally freer and not stiff. If you should find yourself working among people who are mainly or completely Belgian, then you will probably find the atmosphere more restricted. The reference to forms of address and shaking hands, mentioned

Work and Business

in the previous chapter, is especially valid in office and all business relationships. Some clerical and secretarial staff who have worked together for some time may be on first-name terms and may use the *trois bises* (three pecks on alternate cheeks) as a greeting instead of a handshake.

The social security payments made in another EEC country provide immediate coverage for the contributor in Belgium. Anyone not having contributed previously to such a scheme has to wait six months before being able to make any claim. Whether you are considered as a manager or a worker, if you take time off because of sickness you will need to obtain a doctor's certificate. Normally, this should reach your employer on the second day that you are not at work. (The health system is dealt with in greater detail in Chapter 8.)

Another social security benefit available to contributors in Belgium is a generous family allowance payment. It is paid to the wife for each child up to the age of fourteen and for each child up to the age of twenty-five who is continuing his studies or serving an apprenticeship at a recognised institution. The amount received depends on the age of each child and the number in the family. At the moment, the family allowance can still be claimed for a child who is being educated abroad, although there is talk of ending this agreement.

A pregnant woman can apply for a maternity allowance from the sixth month of her pregnancy. Payment is made starting from two months before the expected date of confinement. As for the family allowance, the amount paid for the birth depends on the number of children in the family.

If you have three or more children, you qualify as a 'large family' (*famille nombreuse*) and are entitled to special prices in certain stores, on public transport, and at other places.

Your social security payments also entitle you to claim unemployment pay if you are out of work. While criticised locally as being abused, the Belgian system is nevertheless subject to much tighter control than that in Britain. To qualify, it is necessary to sign on immediately and to report on a daily basis at hours indicated by the authorities. The checking-in time is never the same for any two consecutive days running and is only known the day before, which cuts down considerably the chances of moonlighting. Payments amount to 60 per cent of the gross salary, with a ceiling that varies according to the type of work.

While everyone who works must contribute to the social security system, only the employed can benefit fully from it. Self-employed people, usually known as 'independents', are not allowed unemployment money if their work fails, family allowances are lower and paid quarterly instead of monthly and medical coverage is minimal.

Belgium's Economy
Less than 5 per cent of the working population is engaged in agriculture, which leaves a large number of people involved in industry of one type or another. The country has very few natural resources and, with the exception of coal, is obliged to import virtually all of its raw materials. Belgium's industries, however, have a production potential that is far in excess of its own needs. Thanks to these two features, Belgium is able to export 60 per cent of its GNP, which is one of the highest figures in the world, if not the highest. The major industries are metal manufacture, basic metallurgy, food and beverage, chemicals, textiles, non-metallic mineral products, wood and coal-mining.

Belgium has much to offer investors and goes out of its way to welcome them. In fact, the number one investor nation is the United States. One of Belgium's most important assets is that it is extremely well located, at the hub of Europe. It has a highly developed internal and overseas communications network, both on land (rail, road, water and telecommunications) and in the air. The administrative headquarters of the European Community, NATO and SHAPE, as well as numerous satellite organisations, means that, despite its small size (30,513sq km (11,780sq miles)) and relatively low number of inhabitants (9,857,721), it commands an important position in international business.

Another asset that prospective investors find especially appealing is that it is relatively easy to find suitable premises for renting or for purchasing, both in cities and

Work and Business

in industrial zones. The same is true, too, for private accommodation, which means there are few problems in relocating any of the workforce.

The local labour force is highly skilled and particularly orientated towards modern high-productivity industries. In general, relations between top management and employees are good, and unions co-operate with employers in an effort to save production and jobs. There are few regulations that restrict business and those that do exist are mostly in the sectors of insurance, banking, leasing, transportation, pharmaceutical products, food and drugs.

VAT (TVA/BTW) is charged on all goods in Belgium, even on second-hand items, and on some services. The rate applied depends on the nature of the item: 6 per cent is charged on goods considered as necessities; 17 per cent for 'privileged' goods (that is, certain goods and services of particular economic interest — coal, fuel, laundry, etc); 19 per cent is the standard rate; 25 per cent is charged on luxury goods (such as cars, boats, television sets, etc) and 33 per cent on super-luxury goods (such as furs).

Conditions of sale must be made clearly known to the purchaser and, if any dispute occurs, the Belgian courts will generally require proof of the fact that the buyer has had knowledge of the conditions, has understood them and accepted them.

There are certain activities that are subject to specific regulations and require prior authorisation before starting up in business: these include banking, insuring, financial leasing, transporting and road haulage, stockbroking and commodities, selling of meat and some other foodstuffs, and travel agent activities. Also subject to special requirements are some of the professions (lawyers, doctors, and certain types of auditing).

Banking
Brussels is the Belgian banking centre. In 1984, over 80 different banks were located in the country with 3,656 branches. Of these branch offices some 420 are situated in the greater Brussels area and, when you visit the capital, you can well believe it. Banks seem almost as numerous as restaurants!

Work and Business

About a third of the banking companies are representative offices of worldwide financial institutions: Barclays, Lloyds, Midland and International Westminster all have offices in Brussels, and Lloyds and International Westminster have branches in Antwerp as well. Many of the big American banks are here, too: Bankers Trust Company, Bank of America, Chase Manhattan, Chemical Bank, Citibank, Continental Illinois, IB Financial Corporation, Manufacturers Hanover Trust and Morgan Guaranty Trust.

For personal banking and everyday company business, however, you will be better off using a Belgian bank that can serve your needs close to your home or office. There is a uniform system of numbering utilised by all the Belgian banks which enables one to see at a glance the name of the bank and the customer's number. This means that, when making a transaction, it is sufficient to give just the account number (always twelve figures) without quoting the name of the bank and the branch. There is a built-in control number which will eliminate an erroneous transaction.

Belgian banks offer a sophisticated method for transactions between accounts (business and private), the 'virement', which withdraws money from the account of the person paying and deposits it in the receiver's account, whether or not the two accounts are at the same branch or even at the same bank. The person paying draws up the transfer form, giving his name, address and account number (usually pre-printed by the bank), the receiver's name, address and account number, any reference, the amount (all taken from the bill), and the date; he signs it and deposits it at his own bank, keeping a duplicate for reference. The transaction is confirmed on the next statement.

All current account cheques can be used in conjunction with a Eurocheque card which enables the holder to cash a cheque up to the amount of BF7,000 in any Belgian or European Bank, with the exception of East Germany and several North African countries. Eurocheques are acceptable in most Belgian shops, hotels and even in taxis, and are also accepted by many hotels and shops in Britain, Holland, Luxembourg, West Germany, Finland, Switzer-

41

Work and Business

land, parts of France and Andorra. Belgian Eurocheques are written in the currency of the country in which the cheques are being drawn.

Some Eurocheque cards are combined with, or can be obtained in addition to, a cash card such as Mister Cash or Bancontact. The latter can be used on a twenty-four-hour basis seven days a week at a large number of cash-dispensing points throughout the country. It is possible to pay in some supermarkets and petrol stations with these cash cards, the payment being made immediately by direct transfer from your account to that of the seller. This facility is expected to be more widespread in a few years.

Bank statements can be received on a daily, weekly or monthly basis depending on the volume of your transactions. The cost is relatively low for this service and can be even cheaper if you pick up your statements from your branch. Cheques and 'virement' forms are never returned but the details are recorded on your statement.

Standing orders are probably not used as much as in Britain. They can be arranged for paying bills from utilities – telephone, electricity, gas, water – and rent. Many people, however, prefer to make their own payments since several of the services will cut you off quickly for non-payment and, should the bank overlook making your payment, you may find yourself without telephone or electricity.

When transferring money from or to another country, there are two rates that can be applied: the commercial rate and the free rate. The first is the one that will be applied to your business transactions and the second is the one that will be used when you buy foreign currency for your holiday. Buying foreign currency over the counter can be an expensive business as there is normally quite a difference between the buying and selling rate.

Belgian banks offer other services such as overdrafts, loans, financing, stock-exchange transactions and safe-deposit services. When organising a loan or a financing agreement, it is advisable to check with several institutions to see what is on offer. For example, if you wish to buy a car and do not want to pay cash, you can ask the bank for its terms. Most of the larger car companies have an arrangement with a finance house even if they do not have their own financing department. You could also check with another bank or an independent finance house. One very important point to note, however, is that the figure you accept will remain the same for each repayment you need to make. It will not go up or down with the bank rate.

The Belgian post office offers a type of banking system for making payments and receiving monies which is interest-bearing. Accounts are numbered according to the banking system and all start with 000-.

Brussels and Antwerp have stock exchanges. Shares are either bearer or non-bearer and all interest and dividends are subject to a 25 per cent tax when collected in Belgium. It is possible to buy Belgian stocks, shares and bonds, as well as some issued by other countries, over the counter in your bank. Several of the well-known stockbroking companies have offices in Brussels, too.

Income Tax
Income tax is deducted automatically at source. All residents of the country (that is, any individual who has his domicile or centre of vital interests here) are liable to pay tax. Agreements exist between Belgium and Britain and between Belgium and the United States over the double taxation of their nationals, and so, Britons and Americans have only to pay tax once on their income. Each year an official of the Internal Revenue Service visits Brussels and holds meetings arranged through the American embassy at which US citizens can obtain an updating of the fiscal situation and receive help in filling in their US tax return.

The basis on which your Belgian income tax is assessed takes into account the total net earnings from all sources. For fiscal purposes, the incomes of both husband and wife, where they are living together, are combined, except in the case where their joint total income does not exceed BF750,000.

Personal income tax is payable on income from four different categories: immovable or real property; movable or personal property; remuneration from an occupation or business; and miscellaneous sources. If you own property in Belgium, you will pay tax on it whether you live in it or it is leased to someone else.

Work and Business

Movable or personal property consists of dividends or interest derived from stocks and shares, government securities (except for those carrying a legal provision for tax exemption), bonds, debt-claims, loans, savings or bank deposits, and income from invested capital or the renting of movable property.

The money you earn from your work, whether it is in terms of a salary, wages, or a fee, is subject to tax, as are the profits you may derive from some business, any remuneration you receive as an active partner of a partnership, and any other income received from profit-making activities. Pensions and other such payments are also subject to tax.

There are certain exceptions to the tax you pay on your remuneration. For example, if your employer reimburses the amount you incur each day by travelling to work, this sum is exempt up until a certain amount. In some cases, certain benefits produced by preferential conditions offered by an employer on mortgage loans are subject to exemption, as are some allowances, pensions and benefits.

Miscellaneous income encompasses much: from alimony and similar support payments, to awards and subsidies paid to scientists, authors or artists by public bodies or official non profit-making organisations.

No tax is paid by anyone whose taxable income does not exceed BF100,000. From that amount until the next tax level (at present BF750,000), the amount paid is fixed by royal decree and is not more than about 33⅓ per cent. Over and above this amount, the income is divided into slices with a different, rising percentage applicable to each slice. The ceiling currently applies to F4 million and over, and in no case can the total tax paid exceed 67.5 per cent of the taxable income. As from fiscal year 1987–90, the tax rates will be subject to a 2.25 per cent indexation calculated on the four years.

As far as personal reductions are concerned, there is an allowance made on the amount of income taxed for spouses, whether or not they are both working. The amount varies according to the income level and whether one or both are earning money. There are reductions, too, for other members of the family who do not earn more than a certain amount each year. The amount allowed for children depends on the number in the family.

There are reductions, too, for other dependants, disabled people with a minimum of 66 per cent disability, people living on their own with a dependent child, newlyweds, and the death of a spouse.

There is special tax treatment for some foreign executives; the details of such advantages should be explained to you when the financial arrangements relating to your move to Belgium are first discussed.

The Belgian tax year for the private individual is a calendar year, with the distribution of tax papers beginning around March or April of the following year. The papers are normally sent out in alphabetical order (except for very recent qualifiers) and so those high up alphabetically will receive their declarations first. If your name happens to be at the end of the alphabet you will probably receive your papers in the summer. A last date is indicated on which these forms must be returned duly filled in. The delay given is normally from a month to six weeks, and you can ask for an extension if you have a plausible reason for doing so (for example, you were out of the country for most of the period). It is the taxpayer's responsibility to file his tax form and, if the relative documents have not been received, he should request them from the nearest tax office. Failure to return tax forms on time will incur a fine.

The income tax declaration forms are vast documents accompanied by copious explanatory notes. Most foreigners find it easier and simpler to engage the services of an accountant to fill them in. It is said that there is no one person in the country who knows and understands all the various laws relating to taxation and their implications. Certainly different interpretations can be put on many of the finer points.

The declaration takes into account the tax already deducted from your income at source. However, it does not necessarily mean that that amount is correct as it may not take into account other sources of income earned by the family. If a married woman works, it is highly likely that there will be adjustments to be made. It has already been explained that, unless their joint annual income is

Work and Business

under FB750,000 (for 1985 earnings), a husband and wife will be taxed together, which is commonly known as 'accumulation'. For this reason, few married expatriate women work as income tax rates in Belgium are among the highest, if not the highest, in the world. Both husband and wife (in her maiden name) must sign the tax declaration.

Tax reviews for private individuals, as well as for companies, are common, particularly if the tax department does not fully understand your work or if you are making an unusual claim (for non-resident tax concessions, for example). The Belgian tax authorities do not take the point of view that the private individual does not normally cheat because his return has been filled in by an accountant. To have an accountant to explain why certain deductions have been claimed and for him to give his interpretation of the relevant laws at a tax review is a great advantage.

In addition to the set amount of income tax you will have to pay on your salary to the state, there is a communal or council tax which is also based on the amount of income you declare. This varies from commune to commune with the lowest now being about 6 per cent. For employees fiscally considered as non-resident, the communal tax is fixed at 6 per cent, irrespective of the commune in which they live. The commune tax pays for the refuse collection, street cleaning, town council and local amenities.

Some months after submitting your declaration and when the taxman has made a general check of your return, you will be sent a computerised breakdown of what has been assessed and how it has been calculated. At the bottom it will state how much still has to be paid or how much you are due to be reimbursed. You will have two months to pay before fines start to be imposed. On the other hand, if you are due to be reimbursed, a date will be given as to when you can expect to see that money. Repayment comes in the form of a cheque on the postal giro system and, since both spouses sign the tax declaration, both spouses must sign the cheque and proffer their identity cards for authentication in order to receive the money from the post office.

Work and Business

The fact that you have received the taxman's computerised breakdown and, perhaps even a refund, does not mean that he has accepted finally that year's declaration. It can be reviewed at any time within the next three years for general error and up to five years later in the case of fraud.

Wills
It is advisable to have a will since the laws of Belgium and those of Britain and the United States are, in most instances, substantially different with respect to the persons who would be entitled to the property on death. In Belgium, a surviving spouse is, in general, granted only a *usufruct* with respect to the deceased's estate. It passes to the children on her death. A child cannot be disinherited or one child favoured more than another, and, where there are no children it is divided between the husband's family. This division of the property often makes it extremely difficult to sell.

Specifically About Luxembourg
Employment
Being a much smaller country, there are fewer jobs available, of course. If you do not have employment when you arrive, you will find job advertisements sometimes published in the English weekly *Luxembourg News Digest*. Alternatively, you could look in one of the national daily newspapers, such as the *Luxemburger Wort*. In addition to the American Chamber of Commerce directory, mentioned above, the American Embassy in Luxembourg can provide a list of American companies with offices in the country.

Work permits are needed by all non-EEC nations wanting to take up employment. It is the employer who will make the application.

The working week is normally of forty hours duration and there are ten statutory paid days off each year. In addition, all employees are entitled to twenty-five days holiday per year.

Social security is deducted at source, as in Belgium, but the amount of payments in the case of unemployment is different. In Luxembourg 80 per cent of the gross salary is

Work and Business

paid, provided that this does not exceed 250 per cent of the national minimum salary.

Luxembourg's Economy
Strangely enough, Luxembourg has developed its heavy industry even though it has neither coal-mines nor coke-ovens. Nor are its mineral deposits very abundant and they do not yield high-grade ores. Yet this powerful, modern industry constitutes the basis of the Grand Duchy's economy. It has a decisive influence on the country, not only because of the size of the workforce it employs and the amount of capital invested in it, but also because it is a vital stimulus to the Grand Duchy's economic development.

There is a heavy dependence on foreign trade, which is encouraged even with the amount of VAT charged on consumer goods. The government maintains a definite policy of holding VAT rates slightly below those of neighbouring countries, thus enticing the Germans, French and Belgians to purchase goods in its country. The standard rate is 12 per cent with reduced rates of 6 and 3 per cent applying to some goods and services considered to be essential, such as public transport, various foodstuffs, fuels and pharmaceutical products.

Since the end of the last century, Luxembourg's economy has rapidly developed into an industrial one which has resulted in extensive recruitment of foreign workers. The number of foreign residents now exceeds 26 per cent of the population of 365,000. This is the highest proportion of foreigners in any EEC country.

Its economic structure and its geographical position have necessarily led Luxembourg into a close co-operation with other countries. It joined the German 'Zollverein' in 1842 only to withdraw at the end of World War I and to turn to Belgium instead. The Belgo-Luxembourg Economic Union still exists and, in the meantime, a further economic union has been formed with the addition of the Netherlands. The Grand Duchy is a founding member of the three European communities: The European Coal and Steel Community, the EEC (European Economic Community) and the EURATOM (European Atomic Energy Community).

Brussels is the headquarters of 841 international institutions and organisations, making it the world's second international city. One of the reasons for this concentration is the presence of four European Community institutions: the Commission; the Council of Ministers; the Secretariat of the European Parliament which meets in Strasbourg and in Luxembourg but which is also located in Brussels; and the Economic and Social Committee. The Berlaimont, pictured above, is just one of the Community's buildings in the Capital of Europe (*Belgium National Tourist Office*)

Work and Business

The country plays a more and more prominent role as an international finance centre. Numerous banks and leading investment trusts have settled in the capital as a consequence of the specific fiscal system which dates back to 1929 and favours holding companies. It can now claim to have the greatest banking concentration in the EEC.

Banking
The system of banking differs little from that of Belgium. However, where certain bank charges do exist in the other country, none exist in Luxembourg.

Income Tax
Tax returns must be submitted by 31 March for the previous tax year which ends on 31 December. There are three tax rates which, basically, are for single people, married couples without children and married couples with children. The rates rise most steeply up to the maximum of 57 per cent for taxpayers in the first group, less steeply for those in the second group, and even more gradually for those in the third group. Non-residents are classified under the second group but, in their case, the average effective rate of income tax on total taxable income may not be less than 15 per cent.

There are no special rules applicable to foreigners working in Luxembourg.

Lace-making is a centuries-old tradition in Bruges where it is still possible to see some ladies sitting at their cottage doorways on fine days, niftily manoeuvring the bobbins to create the patterns passed down from generation to generation. The art started to die out a few years ago but the local authorities, which are more conscious of their heritage than most Belgian cities, moved fast to create a lace school and to encourage young people to learn the skill (*Belgian National Tourist Office*)

5
Where to Live

Accommodation in Belgium is generally easy to find and of a high standard, whether you are looking for something modern or for the character of a period building. Since there is so much on the market, it is worthwhile to resist taking the first place that answers your basic requirements and to look around instead, compare several properties, prices, areas and the amenities available to you in each commune or council.

But before you start looking for a place to live you need to make a few decisions, such as whether you prefer the slower, probably quieter, ways of country life or the bustle and all the activities of being in a town; whether you would be happier in a house or in an apartment; and whether you intend buying or renting.

Generally speaking, married couples, especially those with children or those who are keen gardeners, prefer to live in the country. One tremendous advantage which comes from Belgium's small size is that there are plenty of possibilities for living in rural surroundings while being still within a few minutes' drive of the nearest city centre. Unfurnished houses and homes to buy are easy to find in such areas but the chances of finding apartments or furnished accommodation away from the major cities are not so good.

Single people, couples where both partners work, or families that expect to stay for a very short time often take furnished or unfurnished flats in the city. These can be in old houses that have been renovated to create separate accommodation or in modern apartment buildings, varying in size from a few units to large high-rise complexes of several hundred homes.

If your stay will be relatively short or if you are going to live a bachelor existence and travel outside the country a

Where to Live

great deal, a service flat may be the best answer. There are a number of these in the Brussels area and not all are in the heart of the business centre. You will find them advertised in the local English press and in the Yellow Pages of the telephone book together with hotels. They go under a variety of titles: residence, aparthotel, flathotel or some just give a name and mention a rate per week or per month.

Some people prefer to stay in a service flat, too, for the first few weeks of their stay, so that they can take their time looking for somewhere to live permanently, without the feeling of being rushed and unsettled in the less personal atmosphere of a hotel. Likewise, when leaving the country for good, it is often easier to move into such accommodation while going through the paperwork involved in winding up your affairs.

There are several points you will probably want to take into consideration when selecting an area in which to live and, obviously, the first is going to be how easy it is to travel to work. If you do not wish to use a car each day, you will need to check out the various possibilities for the length of time involved in taking the metro, tram, bus or train and, perhaps, even a combination of public services. On the whole, communications are extremely good, even for the person driving in to work in the city each day, although parking in the centre of a town may prove difficult.

Of course, if your work involves a considerable amount of travel by road, rail or plane, you will want to live somewhere with relatively easy access to your point of departure. The marvellous motorway network is a boon to all drivers and, as far as travel by rail and plane are concerned, mainline stations often have parking facilities where you can leave your car. All the major airports have adequate space available at a reasonable cost.

Another consideration when making your selection is very likely to be the proximity of shops, especially if you do not drive a car or are hesitant about driving on the Continent. This presents little problem in Belgium where communities are usually well served with a good variety of local stores, and major shopping centres are but a short metro, bus or train journey away. There is generally at

Where to Live

least one supermarket within easy reach of most communities and, depending on the size of the local population, there may be two or even three.

A major factor for parents with school-age children or toddlers who will be attending a play school or nursery school will be how much time is likely to be spent delivering and collecting them each day from their classes. Most primary and secondary schools, both Belgian and foreign institutions, do have a bus system but you need to be on or near to their routes in order to take advantage of these.

Language could also be an important consideration if you intend residing outside Brussels, in Brabant province where the language spoken is either French or Dutch; or in Wallonia (French only) or Flanders (Dutch only). If you want to send your children to a local Belgian school, rather than one of the foreign institutions, and are living in a commune in which the language is not the one you have chosen for your children's education, you will have to send them to another commune, which will probably involve arranging transportation yourself. Non-Belgians are allowed to send their children out of the commune to be educated at state schools, but Belgians are only able to do so if they comply with certain requirements. There are six areas around Brussels (known as *communes à facilités*) which are Dutch but where French can be used in official communications as well: Drogenbos, Kraainem, Linkebeek, Sint-Genesius-Rode, Wemmel and Wezembeek-Oppem. However, if your child is not French-speaking, he will have to be educated in Dutch if he attends a state school in one of these areas. (Education is discussed in Chapter 7.)

Those who are regular churchgoers or are interested in community activities will probably want to be relatively close to such centres. Or perhaps you have a specific sport that you practise regularly and so you would like to be within easy distance of suitable facilities. How you pass your leisure time should also be taken into consideration when choosing an area in which to live.

Of the nineteen Brussels communes, the ones most favoured by expatriates are Ixelles, Woluwe St Lambert, Auderghem, Boitsfort and, to a lesser extent, Uccle. Both

Where to Live

Ixelles and Uccle are large communes and quite densely populated. Ixelles is very mixed with parts that are old and elegant and others that are modern. The old and new buildings of Brussels Free University are situated in this commune so there is a strong student community as well. Woluwe St Lambert and most of Auderghem are modern and are connected by the River Woluwe. Boitsfort is a mixture architecturally and is particularly known for its roads of flowering cherry trees in the spring, spectacular enough to be mentioned as an attraction in the Michelin guide book. Fewer English-speaking people live on the north side of the capital (Molenbeek and the outlying villages of Meise, Zellik and Wemmel), although there are some very attractive neighbourhoods there, and prices tend to be slightly lower. Now that the metro has extended out in that direction, they are easily reached.

In the green belt surrounding Brussels, Tervuren is a village very popular with the British because that is where the British School of Brussels is situated and the British Primary School is not far off at Vossem. Overijse, and its hamlet of Jezus-Eik (known as Notre-Dame au Bois to the French-speaking community), and Kraainem all have fair-sized British communities since they, too, are, relatively close to these two institutions. Some British families do live out at Waterloo, but the foreign community there is mostly American, despite Waterloo's historical connections with Britain, because St John's International School is located there and the Brussels International School at Boitsfort, another American institution, is within easy reach on the ring road.

Town houses are not so readily available because it has become fashionable and lucrative to knock down old buildings and replace them with blocks of flats. The older ones still to be found in the heart of Brussels are either small and narrow, often without garages, or they are large and lofty, elegant mansions with double gates (as part of the façade) that lead to the main entrance of the house at the side, and then through to a courtyard or garden where there may be a garage. Both types will often be wedged into a row of other dwellings of extremely varied architecture, rarely with two façades the same. It is also rare to find front gardens to these properties, although many

Where to Live

hide delightful walled open spaces, and even other houses, behind them.

In the newer residential areas of towns, houses are also often built with adjoining side walls and sometimes have their entrance, garage, cellars and perhaps a downstairs cloakroom on one level, while the living accommodation is above, including kitchen on the first floor with bedrooms and bathroom. In certain newer suburbs and rural areas, houses often stand alone or are semi-detached. It is not uncommon, either, to see a house standing alone with one or both sidewalls obviously unfinished. This is usually done when the owner is hoping that someone will build on the adjacent site and use his wall, which will allow the costs to be shared.

Houses are classified in a variety of ways. A *villa* is a detached property: a bungalow or a house with more than one storey but standing in its own garden; it can be small or large. A *maison de maître* is an elegant town house with at least three floors, often terraced, and often with a garden behind. A *fermette* is generally a small rustic-style house, either authentic or of modern construction, built on one floor with perhaps the addition of a room or two in the roof. A *bel-étage* is a terraced suburban house with the garage, entrance, cellar and central heating unit at ground-floor level, or slightly below ground-floor level, with kitchen, living-room and downstairs toilet on the first floor. The bedrooms and the bathroom are situated on the second floor.

Houses often have cellars and modern constructions frequently have garages with direct access into the building. Shutters, whether they are the type that open outwards to lie flat against the wall in daytime, or are the drop-down variety built into the construction, are common at ground-floor windows and even on some doors.

In rural areas not all properties are connected to a public sewage-disposal system. These will be served by septic tanks that need regular attention, usually on an annual basis.

Gardens and land are measured in hectares and ares. An acre is equal to 40 ares, so a property of 12 ares is already a fair size if you intend to maintain the garden

Where to Live

yourself. Properties on most housing estates have gardens of about 6 ares. Gates to front gardens or garage driveways are not nearly as common as they are in Britain.

To qualify for the term 'apartment' a flat must have at least one separate bedroom. 'Flats' and 'studios' are bedsitters. Beware of advertisements for 'studios', normally with the word printed in capital letters, and sometimes preceded or followed by a number, as they are let usually only to couples and by the hour.

Modern apartments are generally spacious and very well equipped with many fitted cupboards, a cellar (either individual or communal) for storage and large sitting-cum-dining-rooms known as the 'living'. (It is not uncommon to find 'high standing' written in property advertisements. This means neither that it is built on high ground nor that it has over twenty floors, but that the standard is high.) Kitchens come 'equipped', 'installed' and 'super-equipped'. The first generally means that there is at least one sink (often there is a double sink) and cupboards built in. 'Installed' usually indicates that there is a cooker and a refrigerator as well, and perhaps more. A 'super-equipped' kitchen can contain dishwasher, washing-machine and drier and even a breakfast corner in addition.

'Night halls' are features of larger apartments with several bedrooms and are often cut off from the general living area by a door. Many modern apartments have balconies, and penthouses are not uncommon.

Modern apartment buildings generally have garages either built underneath or behind. These can be of a communal nature, where you have a reserved space, or they can be individual units with their own separate doors. A certain amount of parking space is usually available on the grounds for the use of visitors.

Even relatively small buildings will probably have one or two lifts serving all floors and, in more luxurious establishments, these may stop actually in the apartment. There are very few blocks of apartments that do not have a 'parlophone' system that allows you to talk to anyone ringing your doorbell at the ground floor entrance and to let them into the building without having to go down yourself. In addition to this security system, many build-

Where to Live

ings are locked at night and some at weekends.

It is usual to have a caretaker or janitor to take care of the communal areas of the building for tasks such as rubbish disposal and the day-to-day running of the property. Since apartments are often individually owned and the building is not normally owned by one person or organisation, there will be an owners' association that meets regularly and has a set of statutes in much the same way as a business. The association appoints a manager to represent it legally in such cases as communal insurance, for overseeing any work commissioned by the association and for paying the relevant bills. Usually, the outside part of the building and the property, the communal areas and anything to do with the construction are the collective responsibility of the owners. The occupier, whether he is tenant or owner, of each apartment becomes responsible for the property once he is inside his own front door.

Houses and apartments generally have central heating which is either gas-, electricity- or oil-fired. Some accommodation has open fireplaces in the 'living', but not all are designed to work! In recent constructions it is usual for a cloakroom to be situated off the main entrance hall.

Whether you intend to buy property straight away or rent, you will find that there are several ways of looking for accommodation. Probably the most effective is to select the district in which you want to live and to drive through the streets you like reading all the relevant 'To Rent' or 'For Sale' signs displayed. The sign will clearly display whether the property is an apartment or a house as this is not always obvious. The description will give you an idea of the size of the property being offered and, usually, a quick telephone call to the number given will tell you how much it costs and when it will be empty. If you are interested in seeing it, you can then make an appointment to visit. Do not expect to be able to view a property without an appointment since legally, the occupier can choose two times each week at his convenience when it can be shown to prospective tenants after giving notice.

Alternatively, you can contact an estate agent, and start reading the 'To Let' or 'For Sale' notices in the local press or looking at advertisements in local shops in the area in which you would like to live. At any rate, the time is certainly not wasted driving around the streets as it will familiarise you with several areas and give you an opportunity of seeing which ones you prefer and which ones best meet your requirements.

Estate agents do advertise certain properties in publications that they think will be read by prospective buyers and, in particular, the Brussels free, door-to-door newspaper, *Vlan*, is one popular place. More exclusive properties are advertised in *L'Eventail* and *L'Evénement Immobilier*. The English-language *Bulletin* also contains an important classified advertisement section on housing.

Estate agents abound and were only recognised as a profession by the government in the summer of 1985. The qualifications have yet to be laid down for those setting up as estate agents and so you would be best advised to go only to those that are members of the estate agents' association: CIB.

The help of an estate agent, whether you are renting or buying, will cost you nothing: it is the owner who pays the fee. Many agents subscribe to a central computerised bank of properties that have been placed on the market for buying. The treatment you will receive from agent to agent varies. Some will put you on a regular mailing list which gives the basic outlines of suitable properties, and you call them for further details, whereas others may take note of your particular requirements and then propose two or three properties, make appointments and drive you around to see them.

You will probably pay a more realistic price if you do not go to an agent and are able to deal direct with the owner. If you turn to an expert for help, you have to pay for his services, even if only indirectly. Some multinational companies have employees who will help with negotiations over such matters and, if necessary, have a lease checked by a member of the legal profession.

If you want to pay a lower price you would do well to look in the local newspapers, including the free door-to-door publications, and in shop windows in the area in which you would like to reside. A number of the supermarkets and other shops, such as newsagents, now provide boards

Where to Live

on which people can advertise all manner of items for sale, and these invariably include property. When reading the local press you will need to look in French-speaking papers for property in French-speaking communes and Flemish papers for Dutch-speaking communes. Advertisements in English-language publications invariably mean 'international' prices.

Rented accommodation comes furnished and unfurnished, both for apartments and houses, although the latter are less easy to find furnished. If you know that your stay is to be for a short time you may prefer to rent furnished accommodation. Of course, the extent and quality of the furnishing depends on the amount of money you are prepared to pay but, generally includes the furniture, sometimes a television set (televisions are not usually rented here), blankets, pillows, cutlery, crockery and cooking utensils. You will need to supply sheets and pillowslips, and probably this will mean purchasing locally since pillow sizes are normally 60×62cm (23× 24in). Other items which will not be supplied include towels and table linen.

If you rent a house or apartment furnished it will normally be for a minimum period of a year. Shorter periods are sometimes available, although you will probably have to take a service apartment. Unfurnished accommodation is usually rented for a period of three, six or nine years, with nine years being the maximum period. After that the contract needs to be renegotiated.

The lease states the general conditions: amount of rent, maintenance charges (if applicable) and the duration. It may also specify whether or not the premises can be used as a place of work (landlords are taxed higher on business premises than on residential accommodation). In the case of furnished accommodation, it will detail down to the last spoon what the apartment contains.

Some leases include a 'diplomatic' clause which, strictly speaking, applies only to diplomats who are considered likely to be recalled at short notice. The clause, therefore, gives them the right to give ninety days' notice, at any time, by registered mail.

However, the term 'diplomatic' clause is loosely used to describe the section often inserted in leases for foreign businessmen whose departure can be subject to short notice. It will read something like: 'In the event of the seat of activity of the tenant being moved to a place other than Belgium, the present lease may be terminated with three months' notice.' In this case, when breaking the lease, an additional three, two or one month's rent will be charged according to whether the tenant has occupied the premises for one, two or three years respectively.

For a normal three-, six- or nine-year lease, there is no indemnity due when terminating the contract at the end of the given cut-off periods (that is, after three, six, or nine years), but the requisite three months' notice must be given by registered mail *in advance*. However, if a tenant finds another lessee to take over the existing lease without interruption during these three-year periods, and the landlord is in agreement, no indemnity is paid to the owner. Otherwise, to terminate a lease during the three years will cost you the full rent until the date of expiry or automatic renewal.

When renting accommodation, it is normal for the landlord to arrange for a survey of the premises. It is in the tenant's interests to be present since every defect and the condition of equipment will be noted, and anything missed or considered to be damaged may be charged to him on departure. Usually, the landlord and tenant share the cost of the survey since it is to their mutual advantage. A similar survey is made when moving out. If you do not agree with the assessment made, you can call in an outside expert (estate agents will recommend qualified surveyors). This may sound complicated but, on the whole, the system is effective and amicable.

Furnished accommodation is subject to a special furniture tax of 6 per cent and this is calculated on the amount for which you insure your landlord's furniture. Both furnished and unfurnished property has to be insured by the tenant for civil responsibility, regardless of any insurance held by the landlord (see Chapter 6.)

Prior to occupancy, the landlord will generally require a deposit which serves as a guarantee to cover any damage caused by you and to safeguard against your doing a moonlight flit. At one time it was normal for this guarantee (usually calculated as three times the initial

Where to Live

monthly rental) to be handed over in cash; however, today, it is more common for the money to be placed in a blocked account at a bank where you can obtain the interest on it but where the capital can be released to you only with the agreement of the owner. The landlord, however, is not obliged to accept this method. If you pay cash, do make sure that you receive the interest on the deposit.

Leases will be made in the language of the commune in which you reside. If you do not speak the language fluently, it is wise to obtain a reliable translation. (The British Embassy can supply a list of sworn translators.) If you are dealing through an estate agent, it is possible that he can supply the translation for a fee.

Charges in apartment buildings are divided in different ways according to the sophistication of the installations. 'Charges' may include central heating, hot and cold water, running costs (including the caretaker's salary), maintenance charges, and sometimes electricity and gas. They will be divided between the occupiers, taking into account the different sizes of the apartments. Where meters or counters (for example, for central heating) exist, the system is usually fairer. It is also preferable to have individual gas and electricity bills.

Most expatriates tend to rent accommodation since the vast majority are here only for a relatively short time and because, in some cases, to own property in the country would mean relinquishing special tax advantages. It is important to check your status with your financial adviser or accountant before you consider purchasing. The acquisition of property normally indicates full residential status which can mean the loss of special concessions. However, some people, particularly those who are making a career at the Common Market, do take the plunge and either buy property or purchase land and build their own homes.

There is little difference between the type of property offered for sale and that offered for rent. However, leasehold is not known here, and both houses and apartments are generally sold freehold. I have already mentioned that owners' associations exist for buildings belonging to more than one person. All apartment build-

Where to Live

ings have a written 'Basic Rule' which must be given to new owners. This contains information about the land on which the property is built, the construction of the building and the materials used, as well as regulations applicable to all owners.

If you are buying property, you should have a chance to see and read the deeds before making the purchase. The deeds contain extensive details about the land and the construction of the property. When agreeing the purchase you will be expected to sign a document stating that you are familiar with the deeds.

Surprisingly, it is not common to have a property surveyed prior to purchase. Many estate agents work with a surveyor and/or an architect who can survey property. However, his opinion will hardly be unbiased since the estate agent is working for the owner. This work is mostly given to surveyors since they charge less but, in certain cases, it is advisable to call in an architect. Insurance companies can also survey property and, since they are likely to be meeting any claim on policies they have issued, it is in their interest to make a fair assessment.

Should you require help in financing your purchase the institution to which you go (bank, savings bank or finance house) will normally insist on a survey. The amount of your loan will not be calculated on the purchase price but on the lower, expected seizure value if you default and the finance institution is forced to put the property up for a quick sale. You will be expected to put down immediately at least 20 per cent of the purchase price and to pay all the relevant legal bills involved. The duration of the loan will be determined jointly but the monthly instalments will be a fixed amount. It is a good idea to shop around for financing terms as these can vary from establishment to establishment and from month to month.

Since properties have not been selling quickly, you can usually knock the price down a little. When property is sold by an estate agent it is the seller who pays the 3 per cent commission which is subject to 17 per cent VAT.

Property sold through an estate agent or by private agreement costs about 14-15 per cent more than the agreed price by the time solicitor's fees, stamp tax and a

Where to Live

land tax of 12½ per cent have been paid. There is a diminishing scale of charges applicable to both new constructions and existing property; that is, the more expensive the property the lower the percentage you will have to pay in addition to the original price.

Many properties are sold at auctions which are conducted by solicitors who hold the Basic Rule or Deeds for examination by potential purchasers prior to the sale. Property sold at auction often goes for a lower price than if it were to be sold through an estate agent or by a private arrangement, but you will find that the additional costs involved are considerably higher. About an extra 20 per cent of the agreed price will have to be paid for solicitor's fees and charges.

Another alternative is to buy a plot of land and to build your own home. However, to do this it is advisable to have a good architect who can advise you from the outset on the suitability of various plots. New constructions cost about 9 per cent more than the actual buying price by the time the 12½ per cent land tax and solicitor's fees have been paid.

If you are interested in renting, given a week or two of serious searching for whatever type of accommodation you desire, you will certainly have two or three homes from which to choose. Buying may take a little longer, particularly for the time required for the paperwork to go through and especially so if you decide to purchase at auction. If you want to build you will need even more patience and you would be well advised to rent somewhere else in the meantime whilst you find the plot of land you want, the right architect and builder, and wait for your home to be built.

Specifically About Luxembourg

Accommodation is not nearly so easy to find in the Grand Duchy and more difficult in the city itself than in the surrounding countryside. Consequently, it is usually more expensive in Luxembourg city: sometimes by as much as 20-30 per cent over prices in the country. Unfurnished accommodation for renting is much easier to find than unfurnished places to buy. Finding out when

Where to Live

something is available is part of the course. Furnished places, other than studios, are very difficult to come by.

Because of the shortage of housing, because foreigners in Luxembourg do not have the same problems of losing their tax concessions that expatriates have in Belgium, and because the property tax is relatively low, many people prefer to buy land and build their own homes. There are restrictions, of course, on where you can build and where you cannot and the local council or town hall will be able to tell you if the piece of land which you are interested in buying can be built upon and can explain how you should go about applying for permission. You would be advised to use the services of a good solicitor and a good architect both for buying the land and building your home.

It is not the custom to place 'For Sale' or 'To Let' notices in front of properties as in Belgium. The usual way to find a home here is through an agency or by looking at the classified advertisements under *locations* or *Vermietungen* in the main daily newspapers, such as in the *Republicain Lorrain* or the *Luxemburger Wort*.

Leases are generally fixed by periods of three years although it is sometimes possible to negotiate for a shorter length of time. Short-term leases of a few months are extremely hard to come by. In addition to putting down a deposit (which can be the equivalent of one month's rent or more) you will have to pay the agency's fees when an agency has been involved. These are normally the same as an additional one or two months' rent, and so, it is wise to ask at the outset how much is required.

As in Belgium, there are no light fittings, curtains or rods, or carpets in unfurnished homes, and in Luxembourg it is not usual to have kitchen cupboards or any appliances, either. In fact, cupboard space is not very generous. Furnished accommodation does generally include kitchen appliances, however, as well as utensils, dishes, tableware, linen and furniture. Apartment buildings in Luxembourg tend to follow the German style of architecture with windows that can be opened in two directions and a communal laundry room in the cellar.

Apart from Luxembourg city and the surrounding villages such as Strassen and Mamer, most foreigners

Where to Live

either live around Echternach or Esch/Alzette; the first is on the German border, north-east of Luxembourg city and the second is close to the French border, to the south-west.

There are a thousand parks and green spaces within Brussels' limits. Across one of these, the Royal Park, close to the banking centre and many of the ministries, the inhabitants of the Royal Palace (above) keep a watchful eye on what goes on at the other end, in the Parliament (*Belgian National Tourist Office*)

The moated castle of Beersel, first built between 1300 and 1310, lies in the Flemish part of Brabant province, quite close to Brussels. Beautifully restored, it is uninhabited but provides a marvellous chance for children to play at hide-and-seek on the various levels of its three towers which are connected by well-worn ramparts. Close by is another interesting but quite different castle, that of Gaasbeek, which contains some interesting collections of paintings, tapestries and furniture. On a warm summer's day, you should take the time to stop at one of the nearby cafés in the area and sample a glass of local *kriek* or *gueuze* together with an open sandwich of brown bread and creamy white cheese (*Belgian National Tourist Office*)

6
Moving In

Even if you have as much as a month before the date on which you will move into your new home, it is wise to get started arranging connections to public services the moment you sign your lease or contract, since these do take time and a certain amount of organisation. When you were negotiating your lease or purchase you will have found out from the previous occupier if the electricity, gas and water will be left on. In the case of a house where the central heating is oil-fired, it is usually possible to buy the oil left in the tank. It is customary to have services turned off by the supplying company at the time of the departure of the previous occupier. Obviously, the last thing you want is to move in and then find that you have no electric light, no gas to cook by and no heat – particularly in midwinter.

Sometimes, and particularly where the previous occupier has not yet given notification of his departure, it is possible to stop the administrative machinery and to arrange simply for meters to be read. This will save you some money, but probably little time, as you will still need to be present on the day that this operation is carried out. However, it will guarantee that the services are available when you want them and that you can use them should you wish to do work on the premises prior to moving in.

Meters in furnished accommodation must stay in the name of the landlord and so he will often take charge of the arrangements. Where a lease states that payments for water, gas and electricity are to be made to the landlord you should take the meter readings together before you move in. (The price per unit should be mentioned in the lease.)

Moving In

Arranging for Essential Services

If it is up to you to arrange for any of the major services (water, gas, electricity and telephone) to be connected, it is advisable to make the appointment for one day prior to your moving in. As the companies will probably not be able to give you an exact time of the day when they plan to come, take a good book and a flask of coffee and prepare for a long wait. You will be lucky if you can arrange for them all to come at about the same time or even on the same day. But one important word of warning: if you are not there when they arrive you will be charged for the visit just the same, and you will have to start from scratch to request a new appointment. Make sure, too, that when they come to make the connection you have the identity card of the person subscribing to the service as they will want to verify that the person does actually live at that address. If the service is not subscribed to in your name, you will also need a written authorisation allowing you to act for the person who is legally responsible.

If it was not done when you first viewed the property, ask the previous occupier or the landlord to show you where the main controls for water, gas and electricity are located so that you can show them to the companies turning them on and, also, for your own information in the case of an emergency. In many apartments and in some houses there are two fuse boxes: a main one in the cellar or basement and a secondary one upstairs. Incidentally, it is illegal to use fuse wire and an insurance company can refuse to pay out on a claim if a fire is traced to that source. If your fuse box is not one of the modern, trip-switch types then you will need a good supply of various sizes of ceramic fuses sold in ironmongers or do-it-yourself centres.

Bills for these services must be paid quickly, generally within five working days. Failure to do so means that the services will be disconnected and you will have to pay for them to be put back on. It is also possible that you will have to wait for the service to be re-established.

It is usual for water meters to be read on a yearly basis. If you are out when the representative calls a card will be left for you to fill in and return to the company. However, the meter must be read by the company every two years.

Moving In

The average yearly charge for water for a household is between BF1,500 and BF2,000, including VAT. A deposit is paid for the first 30-40m^3 (1,060-1,412ft^3) depending on the commune in which you reside, and this is deducted from the total price. The price per cubic meter (35ft^3) varies from commune to commune. In areas where consumption is high, bills are paid quarterly.

Gas and electricity are supplied by different companies in different areas, and often both services will be supplied by the same company. The landlord or previous occupier will be able to tell you which company is responsible for your building.

Installation work is more complicated than a mere connection and special, heavy-duty wiring may be needed for major appliances such as washing-machines and dishwashers. Gas and electricity companies are not allowed to connect appliances to the mains. It is a plumber in Belgium that you call in for anything to do with the gas, or an electrician for any electrical appliances that you cannot fit yourself. It is not common to earth small electrical appliances as in Britain and the States and, if you want peace of mind, you will have to arrange for this yourself. European sockets are standardised for two-pin plugs with or without earthing facilities.

The voltage in Belgium is mostly 220 nowadays and, therefore, most British 240-volt appliances work satisfactorily but American equipment needs transformers. Items made for 60 cycles will not work satisfactorily on the Belgian 50 cycles.

The gas distributed by public services is natural. Appliances that have not been purchased new in Belgium should be checked as being suitable for natural gas *before* using for the first time. Since natural gas is much stronger than ordinary household gas, it can be highly dangerous to light a gas ring or oven which has not been especially converted or manufactured. Normally, conversion presents no major problem and can be arranged by a reputable company.

Bottled propane and butane gas are used in some country homes where there is no connection to the national gas network, and both can be purchased easily from hardware stores. Holiday homes in particular often

Moving In

rely on this form of gas for cooking. If you are buying propane or butane regularly, stores will generally deliver your order.

If you are moving into a house heated by oil, you will need to find out the size of the tank and put in an order. Normally, companies will deliver within a day or two. It is usual to order always from the same company and so you may wish to contact the company that provided oil to the previous occupiers. Alternatively, you can contact one or two companies advertising in the Yellow Pages of the telephone book and ask for a quotation. It is customary to receive a discount for ordering 2,000 or more litres (440 gal) at one time, and you will probably be given a better price if you pay cash. Some companies operate what they call a budget plan. You pay an agreed amount, calculated on your average consumption, by regular instalments and the company fills up your tank at specific intervals without you having to call them to do so.

In rented accommodation, existing telephone lines and numbers can often be taken over which will reduce the cost and a probable delay in being connected. The big disadvantage, of course, is that you will receive the previous occupier's telephone calls. Since bills are normally sent out every two months, it is advisable to arrange with the landlord when negotiating the lease how the bill for the take-over period is to be settled. Otherwise, if you are not moving in straight away, you can ask for an interim bill (*compte hors echéance*) to be established by the telephone company up until the day you move in and for new bills to be made out in your name. However, at least three weeks' notification is required by the telephone company in order to establish such an account.

The transfer of an existing line is expensive. It can be arranged on the payment of the subscription, the guarantee and a deposit, all of which are subject to 19 per cent VAT. The deposit will be refunded about three months after the termination of the contract. Where the actual telephone instrument is already installed in the apartment or house, the cost is not so much but, nevertheless, not cheap.

The installation of a new telephone line depends on the availability of lines. The delay can be several months

Moving In

where existing exchanges are already overloaded. The charge for installing a telephone is also quite expensive although reduced rates do exist for people over 70 and for the handicapped. Your telephone equipment can be rented from the national telephone company (RTT) or you can purchase it from a private supplier, but it must conform to the official Belgian requirements.

How to go about applying for a telephone is explained in the front of the regular telephone book. You can save time by going in person to the office serving your commune and filling in the papers on the spot. You will need to show your identity card or passport. If you should want to have an unlisted number you must indicate this on your application form. You will be charged a relatively small supplement for the privilege.

The deposit required fluctuates according to the amount of the previous bills. Everyone starts off at BF400 and, the moment you go over this, an additional deposit will be added to the next bill. This is so that the amount of the deposit covers the amount of the last bill at all times. Similarly, if three consecutive bills are under the amount deposited, the difference will be returned to you. Whilst all deposits are returnable on payment of the final bill and on termination of the subscriber's contract, they do not carry interest. Telephone bills must be paid within ten working days. Failure to do so means that the service will be cut and you will be charged for the reconnection.

Some public telephone boxes only take magnetic telecards which can be purchased from post offices or shops usually located nearby. The cost of your call is deducted from the face value of the card each time you use it. Older boxes, often installed in cafés or restaurants, may operate with a token that you have to buy from the proprietor who can charge what he likes for it.

Telephone calls can be made by direct-dialling to anywhere within the country and to most countries in the world. Where a line is connected to one of the older exchanges, it is necessary to wait after dialling the international prefix of '00' for the 'music', which signals that the rest of the number can be composed, before continuing with the country code. The Belgian area coding is very simple: a '0' is applied to the prefix locally

Moving In

which is eliminated when dialling a Belgian number from outside the country. Belgian telephone numbers, apart from special services, are made up of nine figures including the area prefix.

Unfortunately, the signal for a line that is out of order is very similar to that of the regular ringing sound and is virtually indistinguishable to any but the sharpest of ears. Consequently, if your line is cut, callers will assume that you are not in. Equally confusing is the signal that tells you when the telephone exchange has no free lines to let your call go through, as this is very similar to the ordinary engaged signal. It can be highly frustrating if you know that the other person is keeping a line open to receive your call and you cannot dial farther than the local exchange.

You should not take the telephone off the hook for any length of time. If you do and the RTT finds out they will cut the line and, of course, expect you to pay to be reconnected.

In addition to the regular alphabetical listing telephone book there is a commercial, classified 'Yellow Pages' (literally called here, the golden pages). Subject headings are listed at the front in four languages: French, Dutch, English and German, the order varying each year. It has to be pointed out that the English translations cannot always be relied upon and that another language should be consulted if the English listing does not provide the desired help. In some of the smaller regions the two telephone books are combined in one volume whilst in Brussels the 'Yellow Pages' makes up two volumes on its own. Both are delivered free to subscribers and are updated annually.

Local council services are generally good and efficient. City streets are cleaned weekly, and dustbins are emptied at least once a week. Bottle and paper collections are made regularly, or pick-up points are provided. You can find out from your town hall the days on which dustbins are emptied in your area and the dates when other collections will be made during the year. Dustbins or plastic bags must be put out on the street at a convenient point for the dustcarts to pick them up. Should your collection day fall on a public holiday, arrangements will be made for rubbish to be picked up on another day.

Moving In

Moving In
On the day your belongings arrive from your previous residence, you should have little to do but await the van. Most modern apartment blocks, and some of the older ones, as well as some town houses, have pulley systems installed on the roofs so that furniture can be lifted up the outside and delivered through a window. Such buildings usually have only small lifts and stairwells that would be a removal man's nightmare if he had to carry large and cumbersome objects up inside. A more recent innovation is a removable outside lift which replaces the traditional pulley. There is generally a small charge for using this equipment, but the caretaker will explain the details to you and arrange for it to be available on the day you move in.

In Belgium, it is customary to provide beer for removal men and a crate of a not-too-alcoholic brand (but not a weak table one – *bière de ménage* – either) from which they can help themselves when they feel thirsty, will be greatly appreciated. In fact, it is always wise to keep a few bottles of beer handy for any workman you need to employ.

It may be that you do not appreciate some of the wall coverings or colourings in your new home. If it is rented, it will probably be freshly papered and painted, and some landlords will be kind enough to let you have a say in what is chosen. However, should you want to make changes you can, but only within limits. If there is wallpaper on the walls and you want to change it or to paint over it, you will have to get the landlord's written permission to do so. Similarly, if you want to lay wall-to-wall carpeting and the doors are too long you should not go ahead and have them cut off without your landlord's permission or you will be charged at least for their repair when you move out or for new doors if the old ones cannot be repaired without it showing. You will find a good selection of wallpapers and paints and other do-it-yourself products in the new brico centres that have sprung up in recent years.

If you leave your furniture behind and decide to furnish your Belgian home locally, you will find a wide choice of styles and quality, with prices to match. Belgians spend a great deal of time and money on making their homes

Moving In

comfortable and attractive. You may have a preconceived idea of what you want and find something that you like in one of the expensive specialist shops in Brussels' Avenue Louise area. However, if you want to have an overall idea of the styles available, you should drive out to Mechelen (known to the French-speaking part of the country as Malines) where there is a big furniture-manufacturing industry. As you walk around the town you will begin to wonder if they sell anything else there other than furniture. Slightly nearer to Brussels, in Alsemberg, there are a number of relatively large furniture stores, too. Lovers of Habitat or Conran shops will find one or two established here, and prices are not too different from those at home.

There are some enormous warehouse-type stores, usually situated close to motorways, which specialise in all types of household goods and carry a good range of furniture that is often cheaper than the styles offered in town. Some will even rent you a self-drive van to take your purchases home if you cannot pack everything into your car. One Scandinavian chain which has recently opened up is even open on Sunday.

If you prefer your furniture to be antique, you will soon find that the Belgians know the value. However, the main pieces on the market are large and reflect the country's history with distinct Flemish and Walloon styles. Bargains are not easy to come by and, if you want a piece authenticated, you will need to buy from a member of the Belgian Chamber of Antiques Dealers. Brussels, especially around the Sablon where the weekend antiques market is held, and Antwerp are the main antiques centres.

There are auctions, too, of varying quality, although one point that will certainly strike the connoisseur is that there are very few specialist sales. Apart from the famous Campo picture auctions that attract dealers from far and wide, and the book sales organised by one or two booksellers, sales given over to a specific subject are very rare. Most auctions contain a wide variety of lots, from porcelain to furniture and jewellery to cutlery. Auctions are usually advertised in the weekend editions of the papers as well as in the monthly magazine, *Arts, Antiques, Auctions*.

If you are not able to afford to furnish the whole of your

home with antiques, or if you have a preference for what the French so nicely term *brocante* – a more elegant word than 'second hand' – there is an organisation situated in Brussels which accepts old furniture and resells it for charity. Called *Les Petits Riens* (in French) and *Spellenhulp* (in Dutch), its vans make collections most days and so the stock is constantly changing. The goods that come in, not necessarily in first-class condition, are off-loaded into an old warehouse and would-be buyers can ferret around to their heart's content.

Belgium is the world's largest exporter of carpets and carpeting, beating even the United States which is the world's largest producer but which has a much larger home consumption. Most of the carpet factories are situated in a region that follows the motorway from Kortrijk to St Niklaas and which, consequently, have given it the name, 'Carpet Highway'.

Specialist carpet and floor-covering stores can be found on the outskirts of many major cities, offering a wide variety of designs and qualities. Carpeting is certainly not cheap, however, and whatever the quality you buy, can represent a sizeable part of your budget for furnishing the new home.

Soft furnishings are generally more expensive than in Britain, too, and the choice is not as big. But one advantage is that in almost every shop where you can buy material it is possible to give the measurements to which curtains should be made up. This will be done relatively quickly, for an extra charge. I have not succeeded in finding the selection of Rufflette tapes here that exist in Britain, and anyone wanting more than the standard design should arrange to have an order sent over.

Small electrical appliances are normally cheaper in Belgium than in Britain. Cookers are not so well equipped: not all have grills, and if they do, it may be in the oven; ovens are usually very small. There are some excellent freezers and refrigerators on the market, but freezer accessories are not so well developed as in Britain (such items as freezer record books, pencils and tape are very difficult to find, if not non-existent). Radios are also quite cheap in comparison with those on sale in Britain but colour television sets are expensive because they are

Moving In

multi-standard, capable not only of picking up the PAL system that Belgium uses but the SECAM system used by France. This is compensated by the fact that most people can pick up at least thirteen or fourteen television stations.

One of the things it is almost certain that your new home will not have is light fittings. The previous occupier may have been kind enough to leave a simple lampshade in the bathroom and, perhaps, in the kitchen and toilets. Apart from that, you will need to buy your own. It is not so usual to find a shop stocking just light fixtures but most department stores will offer a good selection of ceiling, wall and table lamps. It is not easy to find frames in order to make your own shades although there are a number of shops that will make shades to order.

Insurance
In order to insure your household property, it is advisable to go to a broker or agent experienced in handling such requirements for people of your nationality as he will be more familiar with the type of coverage you are used to. He will also be aware of the types of insurance taken out here that you may not be familiar with in your own country.

If you are renting property you need to be covered for tenant liability. Generally, such a policy will cover the cost of reconstruction in case of fire, lightning and explosion. Coverage for damage by storm, water, electricity and breakage of windows can be added. Tenants of furnished accommodation will be expected to take out insurance to cover any damage they might cause to the landlord's belongings. The cost of such a policy will be based on the cost of your rent with the level of coverage being about twenty times the annual rent.

Your own belongings – furniture, household goods, antiques, clothes, jewellery and furs – can be insured against theft from the premises where they are kept. In order to make a claim, the insurance company will require proof of a break-in and money must have been locked away in a drawer, cupboard or safe in order to be reimbursed.

You will need to take out a work accident insurance for anyone you are employing, even on a part-time basis, such as for a cleaning woman, gardener or au-pair. This will not only cover any accident the person has on your premises but will include any incurred on the way to or from work. The premium is not expensive.

There is one type of insurance generally overlooked by foreigners but which is taken out by 90 per cent of all Belgians and that is family liability. It covers any member of the family and household pets for any injury they may inflict on a third party or any damage they may cause to other people's property. Although it is known as 'family liability', single people and couples are strongly recommended to take out coverage. Again, the premium is very low.

Registration

Within two weeks of arriving in Belgium, you must register at the local town hall. (If you have not found accommodation within that time, or if you are living in temporary accommodation, then you must register temporarily at the town hall in the commune in which that accommodation or hotel is situated.) No one can reside in Belgium for longer than three months without such a residence permit and, in fact, you will find it virtually impossible to subscribe to all the usual services such as gas, electricity, water and telephone, or to open a bank account without it.

If you are a British citizen or hold the nationality of another EEC country, you should take with you a valid passport (a British visitor's passport is not sufficient) and three passport-type photographs. You will have to pay a small communal tax and it is possible that you will be fingerprinted. You will be issued with a temporary residence permit valid for three months which is then extended for three months whilst the authorities check you out. You will then be issued with an identity card, valid for five years, which allows you to stay in Belgium and means that your name has been entered in the Register of the Population.

The procedure is slightly different for non-EEC nationals, such as Americans, who can only obtain their residence permit once they have been granted a work permit. Of course, where a family is concerned, it is only

Moving In

the bread-winner who needs to produce a work permit. The other members of the family will be admitted automatically. However, even though your work permit should have been obtained for you prior to arrival in Belgium, you still need to apply at your local town hall for your residence permit within two weeks of arrival. In addition to your passport, those of each member of your family, and three passport-type photos of each person requesting residence, you will also need to show your entry visa or authorisation for provisional sojourn, a medical certificate obtained from a specially authorised Belgian doctor, work permit and a certificate of good conduct and morality (see Chapter 2). The amount paid as a communal tax by non-EEC nationals for the residence permit depends on the nationality of the person requesting it. Here, too, it is possible that fingerprints will be taken. The foreigner's identity card is valid only for one year and has to be renewed before it expires.

Although very young children do not have identity cards, they have to be registered at the town hall nevertheless. Until they are twelve years old they receive a 'name card' which they should carry when they are not accompanied by their parents. From twelve to fifteen years they can have either a name card or a child's identity card, depending on the parents' wishes.

You are legally required to carry your identity card, at all times. Belgian police have the right to hold anyone – including foreign visitors – at a police station, even overnight, if his or her identity cannot be established immediately. And always carry sufficient money – even if you are out jogging or walking the dog.

Licences

Another important document you will require is a Belgian driving licence. You cannot drive on a foreign licence in Belgium longer than a few weeks. In some cases the Belgian one is issued by the town hall, in others by the police, and so it is best to check when obtaining your identity papers which service will supply the driving licence.

If you have a current driving licence from a country issuing a similar document to the Belgian one (Austria,

Denmark, Finland, Great Britain and Northern Ireland, Greece, India, Ireland, Japan, Luxembourg, Norway, Sweden, Switzerland, the United States and West Germany all conform) you will not need to pass the Belgian driving test. You will be required to fill in the application form and take it to your local issuing office along with your current licence and two passport-type photographs. If you are a national of an EEC country, it is quite possible that your previous licence will not be returned to you when the Belgian one is issued. A relatively new EEC regulation stipulates that since, in effect, the licence is being exchanged, the one it is replacing should be sent back to the issuing office. However, it will be returned to you when you move back permanently to the issuing country.

If you are eighteen years old or older, and do not hold a driving licence, you will have to take a written test on the Belgian Highway Code before you may take lessons to drive a car. There are a number of authorised driving schools from which you can take lessons. Before you are granted your licence you will have to take a practical examination as well.

It is not necessary, as long as you are sixteen years old or older, to obtain a licence in order to ride a motorcycle that has a top speed of 25kph (16mph) (Class A). However, if the vehicle is more powerful – with a top speed of 40kph (25mph) – then you will have to take the written test on the Highway Code and you must wear a helmet when riding the motorcycle.

If you wish to ride a motorcycle which can reach speeds of over 40kph (25mph) (Class B), you need to be over eighteen years old and to have taken the written test before you can start driving lessons. Passengers cannot be carried on a motorcycle by a driver who is under eighteen years of age. (The address to write to for full information on the driving test, driving schools and testing centres can be found in Appendix 1.)

You will need a licence for a bicycle if you own one in Belgium. This is obtained from the local commune and comes in the form of a registration plate that must be affixed to the vehicle. There is a small annual charge for the licence that varies from commune to commune.

Moving In

If you have a dog you will need a licence to take it onto the street. This, too, is obtained from the local commune, and the cost varies according to what your council has decided to levy. The tax is paid annually, and you will receive a registration disc that must be attached to the dog's collar and worn at all times outside your property.

There are separate licences for radio and television but these cover any number of sets within the same household. In fact, you receive no document that specifically states you have bought your licence; the second part (B) of your bank transfer form serves as the receipt and can be stamped by the cashier when you hand in the payment demand (part A). Separate payments have to be made for each car's radio, for radio and television sets kept in second homes in Belgium, or for sets that are transported to second homes for use there (even if a licence has been paid for for their use in the first home). The fee is less expensive than that paid in Britain, and the charge for a black and white television licence is a little lower than that for colour.

If you purchase your set here it is normal for the supplier to notify the relative government department of your name and address and for the licence bill to be sent automatically. However, if you bring either a radio or television into the country with your personal belongings, you should notify the relevant department immediately (see Appendix 1 for the address). Cover will be arranged for a few months, and then the bills will follow automatically. One word of warning: Belgium possesses detector equipment.

There is good shooting to be had for which a hunting licence, which is valid for one year beginning on 1 July, must be obtained. This is obtained after you have passed a theory examination and on production of a certificate of good reputation, two passport-style photographs, an insurance certificate, the receipt showing that you have paid the provincial tax and the necessary fiscal stamps covering the cost of the licence.

If you do not intend to shoot on a regular basis, but are invited for a weekend party, your host can obtain for you a *permis de port d'armes*, valid for five days. This is only available to foreign visitors, and the cost is about a

Moving In

quarter of the ordinary hunting licence. You will have to supply a passport-style photograph, insurance certificate and your foreign licence.

The whole question of holding guns for defence purposes is under discussion at present. Licences have been obtainable in certain cases, especially for someone living in an isolated place. A number of deadly weapons on the market, however, do not yet need such a licence, so it is best to check with your local police station as to whether or not any weapon you intend keeping requires such a permit. In any case, it will be your local police who would issue the document.

Some people collect antique firearms as a hobby, and it would be quite natural to start such a collection in Belgium, home of the famous Browning factory in Liège. If a weapon has been rendered harmless, you do not need a licence; however, those that can be fired need a licence and for this you should contact your provincial government. The address for Brabant (Brussels lies in the province of Brabant) is given in Appendix 1.

Fishing is quite an important pastime in Belgium but you will need a licence to fish any but private waters. When you purchase your licence, which is cheap and obtained at the post office, you should take care that you are given the right type. There is quite a variety and one that you purchase in Flanders is not valid in Wallonia.

Specifically About Luxembourg

If you are moving into property in Luxembourg city, the gas, electricity and water are all supplied and connected by one authority, the *Recette Communale*. This also makes life very easy when it comes to bills as well since all the services will be charged on the same invoice. Bills are sent monthly.

Outside Luxembourg city, electricity is supplied by CEGEDEL and bills are issued quarterly. There is no piped gas and so any appliance will need to be built to use bottled gas. For water connections you should look in the local telephone book under *Administration Communale*.

When trying to take over a previously connected telephone line or requesting the installation of a new one, you should contact the PTT. There will be a charge for

Moving In

connection and a monthly rental fee in addition to the cost of calls. Details of the telephone service and the cost are to be found in the front of the telephone book on the green-edged pages.

In fact, the whole of the Grand Duchy of Luxembourg is served by one telephone book which contains far more information than just a listing of names, addresses and telephone numbers. There is all manner of useful information, such as the postal codes for every street in every commune, given in the front. This part is separated by the colour-coding of the edges of the pages. The listing itself is not only alphabetical but also by subject, rather like the 'Yellow Pages' in other countries. It is also remarkable in that it includes the private addresses and telephone numbers of everyone in the land from the prime minister to the humblest worker.

Dustbins in Luxembourg city are emptied twice a week but only rubbish placed in standard dustbins or in bags available from the commune will be taken away. In addition, there are regular collections for throwing away bigger objects. These take place once a month within the city and every three months outside it. The commune issues a circular, listing the dates, to all households.

Whilst most of what I have written earlier in this chapter on furnishing your home is true for Luxembourg as well, there is one very important difference to take into account. Since VAT is lower in Luxembourg, the costs of furniture, carpets, furnishing materials and household goods are cheaper than in Belgium. Taste and styles show a much stronger Germanic influence, too.

As far as registering is concerned, which you must do as quickly as possible, everything that I have written for Belgium applies to Luxembourg with the exception of the title of the certificate of good character, which is called an *Extrait du casier judiciaire*. Non-EEC nationals must apply to the Police des Etrangers at the Ministère de la Justice for the *Authorisation de séjour*. The identity card is issued by your local town hall.

Your driving licence can be obtained by taking a medical certificate issued by a local doctor, in addition to the same type of documents as for the Belgian licence, to the Ministry of Transport.

Moving In

As in Belgium, it is necessary to pass a test in order to obtain a hunting licence. This is valid from 1 August through 31 July and must be renewed annually, for at least eight years, before a licence can be issued without taking a test. Applications should be made to the Administration des Eaux et Forêts.

Fishing licences are issued by the Commissariat de District and are valid for one year throughout the country.

One of the many benefits of living in Luxembourg is that there is no radio or television licence to be bought.

7
Education for All Ages

If you are moving to Belgium with your family, your other major priority, besides setting up your new home, will be to see your child or children established in a suitable school. If your company is paying for the education, as is the case of many expatriate families living here, you will probably opt for one of the 'local' English-speaking schools. If you are footing the bill yourself, you will certainly want to consider the other alternatives since day school here costs about the same as that for a boarder at an independent school in Britain.

Education for children is compulsory. Primary school starts at the age of five or six, but all children must attend by the time they are six years old. It is normal to start at primary school in the September of the calendar year in which the child becomes six years old. In fact, most parents send their children to a kindergarten for at least one year prior to enrolling them in primary school. Both schools are often under the same roof and, in this way, the child is well prepared for what is to come when he or she moves into the serious environment of the primary school.

The move from a Belgian primary to secondary school is made at about the age of twelve. The school-leaving age is sixteen at the present time but may either be raised to eighteen or be lowered once more to fifteen because of the cost involved.

There are certain facilities that are generally provided by Belgian schools and by many foreign ones, too, such as hot meals, for which there is a reasonable charge. For those who prefer to take a packed lunch, soup or coffee are usually available for a few francs. As far as transport is concerned, special school buses are usually available. A charge is made for this facility according to the distance

Education for All Ages

travelled. Students travelling on public transport, whether or not to attend school, may obtain special rates. These concessions are given by the transport system in question (see Chapter 11).

Many schools, both at primary and secondary level, organise supervised homework classes. These not only provide parents with the possibility of collecting their children later from school (a great advantage where both are out to work) but the child can often ask for help from the teacher presiding with the work set. There is a small charge for children taking advantage of this service. In addition to the supervised homework classes, it is usual in Belgian primary schools, and in most nursery schools, for the doors to open at least one hour before the classes start in the morning and for them to remain open until about 6.30pm at the end of the day.

The Belgian academic year begins from about the first Monday in September and continues until the last weekday in June. The beginning of the new school year is a great commercial event with shops selling writing materials and clothes for *La Rentrée/Terug naar School* for weeks before. The holidays taken during the school year, which are never very long, are determined by whether the institution is French-speaking or Dutch-speaking. The autumn term usually ends a day or so before Christmas and the winter term starts a day or two after New Year's Day. The Easter holiday is usually about two weeks. The foreign schools generally keep more closely to this timetable than to that of their own country's academic year but, of course, they are obliged to hold their state examinations on the days prescribed by the respective examining bodies.

Brussels is well served with English-speaking playgroups for young children, and Antwerp has one or two. They are usually run by mothers on a rota basis, in their own homes, for five or six children at a time, and are free. Since they are not run as businesses, and are usually operated by mothers who happen to have a child of that age at that time, it is not possible to name any groups specifically. However, the churches and the women's clubs will certainly be able to put you in touch with the ones being organised for your area.

Education for All Ages

If you would like your child to mix with local, French-speaking children, there are creative playgroups, known as *farandoline*, for infants from one to three years old. Generally the groups meet two weekday mornings, and the children are cared for by a qualified teacher with the help of a mother. There are rarely more than fifteen children in one group and the mothers take turns to help the teacher. There is a small charge. Your local town hall will be able to give you the names of those in your commune.

For the older, pre-primary school child, there are some English-speaking playgroups where attendance is from three to five mornings a week. Creative activities are pursued, and a certain amount of tuition is given in preparation for primary school attendance. The three primary schools following the British education system take children at this stage: the Antwerp English Primary School and Kindergarten and the Brussels English Primary School take them from two and a half years; the British Primary takes them from three years. Of the schools offering an English-language education (either British or American system) through to university entrance, the E.E.C. School of Antwerp (which has nothing officially to do with the European Community) has a kindergarten for children from two and a half years old; the British School of Brussels, the International School of Brussels, St John's International School (at Waterloo) and the Antwerp International School all take children from the age of three. Several establishments in this last group will take children at two and a half years provided they have had their third birthday by 31 December.

Of the Belgian schools especially popular with foreigners, the Ecole Hamaïde takes children from two and a half years old, and the Ecole Internationale 'Le Verseau', at Bierges/Wavre which teaches English starting from kindergarten level, takes them from three years. Children can attend the Lycée d'Anvers, in Antwerp, which is French-speaking, from the age of two and a half years old.

All the schools named charge a fee, and these vary considerably from school to school, and according to whether the child stays for half a day or for a whole day. The foreign schools are all in line with, if not more expensive than, the normal pre-prep school pricing in

Britain. At this stage, the Belgian private schools charge about two-thirds of the price of the foreign ones.

But perhaps your child is older and will be attending primary or even secondary school. What are the chances of giving him a British educational system schooling? At primary level, the establishments offering strictly this type of curriculum are: the Antwerp English Primary School and Kindergarten, the British Primary School (Vossem, near Brussels), the British School of Brussels (Tervuren, near Brussels), and the Brussels English Primary School. The SHAPE International School, which is only open to the offspring of personnel employed at SHAPE, has an English primary section but no secondary school. (The American and Canadian sections offer elementary and high school tuition.) Only the British School of Brussels offers tuition up to British university entrance. This school has over a thousand pupils and caters for all levels of ability. About 80 per cent of the pupils are British, with a wide range of nationalities making up the other 20 per cent.

Parents working at the Common Market or in one of the EC institutions, have the possibility of sending their children to one of the European Schools. Children who do not have a parent working for one of the European Communities are sometimes admitted, provided that there is room for them. There are three European Schools in Belgium: two are in Brussels, in view of the large number of employees in the capital; and there is another one in Mol in the north-east of the country which serves the families of Euratom employees. They follow an education system common to all European Schools and which leads to the European Baccalaureate, a diploma recognised by member state countries and several others, too. Wherever possible, teaching is in the mother tongue, and both the Brussels schools have English sections.

If you are working for the Common Market you do not pay for your child's education at the European School; any parent who is employed elsewhere and for whose child a place can be found at one of the schools, has to contribute a small amount. The cost, however, is nothing in comparison with that for education at the other foreign places of learning.

Education for All Ages

Very few children from non-EEC institutional backgrounds are accepted by the European Schools. However, even parents who have the right to send their children to these schools do not always take advantage of it for the simple reason that the type of instruction provided does not suit every child.

Most schools in Belgium with the word 'international' in their name follow an American educational system. Of these, only St John's International School, a Catholic-ecumenical establishment, will enter pupils for the British GCE examinations, although the basic instruction follows an American syllabus. Another institution primarily following an American curriculum, but also teaching GCE subjects, is the E.E.C. School which has campuses in Brussels and Antwerp. While this establishment's prices are considerably lower than the other foreign schools in Belgium, pupils wishing to receive instruction in order to take the English GCE examinations are charged more than those following the American course. The one Belgian school to offer GCE teaching is the Ecole Internationale 'Le Verseau' but this is only of English; other subjects form part of the Belgian syllabus which is generally followed.

The other places of learning offering an American-based education are the Antwerp International School, Brussels American School, Brussels Christian School, International Christian Academy, International School of Brussels, and the International School of Liège (up until twelve years old). The Brussels American School is a US Department of Defence school and, as such, open only to children of US military and diplomatic personnel and the offspring of other nationalities serving with NATO.

Of these institutions, the Antwerp International School and the International School of Brussels both prepare students for the International Baccalaureate diploma which is now being offered by about 350 schools worldwide. With this diploma, students can enter colleges and universities throughout the world and they have a distinct advantage in the United States. The French school in Antwerp, the Lycée d'Anvers/Collège Marie-José, quite popular with foreign residents, also follows the International Baccalaureate course.

Several schools are looking at the new International General Certificate of Secondary Education examination, a parallel to the new GCSE examination about to be introduced in Britain. However, no definite decisions have been made by the schools as of this writing, and implementation would not be before 1988.

There are also schools offering a German curriculum (the Deutsche Schule Brüssel), a Japanese curriculum (the Ecole Japonaise de Bruxelles), Swedish and Norwegian curricula (Ecole Reine Astrid), a French national curriculum (the Lycée Français de Belgique) and a Dutch national curriculum (the Nederlandse School, Prinses Juliana). Fees vary according to whether or not the institutions are subsidised.

Belgian Education
If you decide to send your child to a local, Belgian school, the instruction will be in the language of the area in which you live, unless you exercise your right as a foreigner to send your child outside your commune to a school of the other language. For information about such schools, the British and Commonwealth Women's Club's area hostess will be able to help you, or you may visit the schools.

Few Americans send their children to Belgian schools, but information is available from the American Women's Club for those interested.

There are two types of state-assisted schools in Belgium: the official ones and the 'free' or 'liberal' ones. The official schools are either financed directly by the state and, therefore, are strictly state schools, or follow the state curriculum more or less and are communal or provincial establishments. Most of the 'liberal' schools are Catholic with just a few non-religious institutions. On the whole, the Catholic schools have a better reputation for discipline and standard of education. The 'liberal' schools receive most of their financing from the state and parents generally have to pay for some amenities, such as writing materials, transportation and certain sports activities. The costs involved are certainly not as high as those at private establishments in Britain. There are some private schools that are fee-paying. Parents wanting their child to have a good foundation in the other main national

Education for All Ages

language will send him to boarding school for a year or so. However, there are not many of these institutions in the land.

Children stay a minimum of six years at primary school, where the curriculum is divided into three two-year cycles. The syllabus puts considerable emphasis on the language used for instruction — either French or Dutch — and on mathematics, which is taught very well. Other subjects in the curriculum are history and geography (from a Belgian viewpoint, of course), science or the study of the environment, religion and physical education.

Parents can choose the religious instruction their child should follow: Catholic, Protestant (which is often more evangelical than in British schools) or ethics, or from any other religion represented in the school. The second national language is taught in the last three years of primary school in Brussels, in the sixth year in Flanders and, optionally, in the sixth year in Wallonia.

Physical education is not so important as in the British curriculum and, normally, only gymnastics and swimming appear on the timetable. However, there is usually an opportunity for children to pursue sports, and team games in particular, on Wednesday afternoons, during lunchtime or even after school. This is the same time that some of the arts can be studied; however, all these activities have to be paid for.

Homework starts in the first year at primary school and continues throughout the child's educational life. Teachers are often more accessible to the parents than in Britain, with an immediate dialogue being established through the child's homework book. The parent has to sign this document to indicate that the homework has been completed, and both the parent and the teacher send messages to each other through it. When collecting the child at the end of the day, parents can generally find class teachers available to discuss progress or they can see them by appointment if a more private interview is required. Parent/teacher meetings are held at least once a year.

The child's knowledge is constantly tested, most often orally. It is usual for children to have to achieve a certain percentage at the end of each academic year in order to move up into the next class. At secondary school, if their results are borderline, they can retake their weak subjects at the beginning of the new school year. If they pass on the second try they can then move up to the next class with the others but, if they do not attain the required results on the second attempt, then they must stay down a year, known as 'doubling'. Primary school children do not retake failed examinations but automatically 'double' if they have not attained the required standard. At the end of their primary school education, usually at the age of twelve, pupils sit an examination set and marked by teachers in their own school. If they pass this examination successfully they receive the primary school certificate.

At this point, special orientation tests set by a psycho-medical-social centre are also given. These are intended to help in the selection of the most suitable branch of secondary schooling to be followed. However, there is no obligation to follow the advice obtained. It should also be taken into account that these tests can prove quite difficult for a foreign child with only a year or two of schooling in Belgium since there is a considerable cultural bias.

A child must move on to secondary school at least by the age of thirteen years and whether or not the primary school certificate has been gained. Usually, however, children make the move at twelve years. Without the certificate, a child wishing to enter a secondary stream either must take a transitional year's course, known as first year B, or must be tested in mathematics and the main language by the chosen secondary school. If the admissions board is satisfied, he passes into first year A. A child who successfully completes the first year B has the possibility of repeating the first year of secondary studies in any branch (that is, in general, in technical or in professional studies), or he can move directly into second year professional studies.

The secondary school system in Belgium is something of an enigma to many foreigners. This is largely due to the fact that there are two systems still in operation: the revised system, known as the *renové*; and the traditional, humanities system. The revised system was made compulsory in state institutions in 1978 and all but about 10 per cent of French-language schools and 30 per cent of Dutch-language schools have adopted the curriculum. It is generally agreed that the revised system has not proved the success that it was expected to be because of the enormous demands that it puts on the teaching staff to provide a much wider range of subjects with all the options that have to be made available.

In the first year of the revised system, a general curriculum is taught which highlights the same subjects as those taken in primary school but which puts emphasis also on the second national language. In addition, there is an opportunity to study Latin, technical studies or art, which may include craftwork such as woodwork or photography, depending upon the school's facilities.

In the second year there is an even greater choice of optional subjects besides those already mentioned, with economics, social sciences and music being added. Optional studies now occupy six hours of the weekly thirty-two hour timetable instead of the two hours in the first year.

By the third year the time set aside for optional studies has increased even more, to ten hours. By the end of this year, pupils are expected to know what they want to specialise in: general studies, technical transition, technical qualification and professional studies. The first three specialisations allow pupils to continue to higher education; professional studies prepares them for a trade, such as dressmaking, hairdressing, woodwork, etc.

The old-fashioned, traditional system gives the child a choice between a general (including the classics, *humanités*), technical or professional studies curriculum. These branches are more rigid than in the revised system, and students choose their options right from the start. Of course, this is fine for children who know where they are going in life but how many really do at the age of twelve?

On completion of the sixth year, students in the *humanités* stream sit the examination for the diploma. This is set and marked by each school, although the syllabus will have been inspected by a special commission. The examinations will be written and oral, with far more oral testing than in British schools. Pupils receiving this diploma and passing the maturity examination are eligible for a place at university or at some specialised learning institution.

Unfortunately, the Belgian system does not make much allowance for even the slightly handicapped. Anybody considering moving here with a handicapped child would be wise to find out first from the foreign schools if they could provide tuition and talk to the Community Help Service to find out what its specialists recommend. The International School of Brussels does have a unit for handicapped children who do not have severe behavioural problems. Obviously, handicapped children and children with learning problems generally have greater difficulty learning a second language than a child without such disadvantages.

When thinking about your child's schooling you should start backwards and bear in mind constantly the type of higher education (if any) the child will need and in what language and in which country he or she will want to receive it. If you can settle on the country to which your child will turn for his or her post-secondary school instruction, then that will dictate to a certain extent the options available to you for the secondary education at least.

It is essential to make sure that the school you choose can provide the best possible teaching and facilities for the type of syllabus your child wishes to follow all the way through school, not just for the first two or three years. It is equally essential that the school is well-established enough to be able to guarantee that this standard will be maintained in the subjects required as long as your child attends.

When considering schools that offer a choice of curricula, it is wise to check that all the subjects your child wishes to study can be followed in the curriculum of your choice. This may make a considerable difference to whatever diploma is awarded on termination of studies and, consequently, may influence the chances of higher education.

One last word of warning. Education today is a commercial business, and you should be just as critical in

Education for All Ages

your choice of school as you would be if you were buying a house or selecting a new car. If you need advice or an unbiased opinion, talk to the Community Help Service which has two professional educational counsellors on its team, one for the American system, the other for British education. The CHS, as it is widely known, was set up by the English-speaking community for the use of the English-speaking community, to deal with all manner of problems, including educational ones.

It is very unlikely that anyone on the point of moving to Belgium will have a child who is about to enter a Belgian university; most British students will opt for a British university and Americans will prefer to enter one of their institutions. However, in view of the fact that you may be considering putting a child into a Belgian school, it might be worthwhile knowing a little about the university system.

Provided the child has completed his or her education at a Belgian school, received the diploma and passed the maturity examination, then a place virtually has to be found at one of the universities, which are either state or liberal institutions. No interview is conducted for a university place prior to registration which takes place on special days. At the moment, it is only in engineering subjects that there is any competition for places at university, although, at some colleges, acceptance does not necessarily mean that the student will follow the course he chooses.

The enrolment fee, together with any tuition fee, are payable on the day of enrolment. Tuition fees are not required of students whose parents reside and have their main occupation in Belgium, if they attend a seat of learning through a bilateral agreement, or if they are post-graduate students from Third World countries. Even if you do have to pay tuition fees, they are much lower than those charged by American universities and less than the cost of a year's sixth form education at one of the foreign schools in Belgium.

Registration usually takes place during August and September, but you need to put in your request for registration as early as possible and usually not later than the beginning of July. The first term starts early in

Education for All Ages

October. It is at the end of the first year that the 'weeding out' begins with those who fail examinations having to retake them before the new year commences or to repeat the whole year. You can normally double a year only once at the same university.

Universities are either French- or Dutch-speaking. In Brussels, it is possible to attend university in either language: at the Université Libre de Bruxelles (ULB) or the Vrije Universiteit van Brussel (VUB), which are basically on two different main campuses although some of the newer buildings are adjacent. Outside Brussels, there are French-speaking universities in Liège, Mons, Namur, Arlon and Charleroi, as well as at Louvain-la-Neuve, near Wavre, which is where the country's oldest university transferred to after the scission caused by language differences in 1968. The Flemings won the day and retained the university they know as Leuven which has been established since 1425. (Many American students study medicine at the Katholieke Universiteit Leuven (KUL) where much of the work is in English.) Other Dutch-speaking universities are situated in Antwerp, Ghent, Limburg, Kortrijk and Wilrijk/Antwerp.

Some specialist courses have lectures in English but the foreign student is expected to have some knowledge of the university's official language. However, it is usual for the relevant supplementary language course to be available for the foreign student.

Studies are mostly divided into two cycles of either two or three years' duration each, and a degree is usually obtained after four or five years. Changing colleges and universities during the course of studies, and even changing curricula, in order to tailor the programme to an educational background that will best suit the profession anticipated, is becoming a feature of Belgian education today. It is common for a student to start at one establishment, then to switch to at least one other and, at the same time, to change the branch, before completing normal academic studies and obtaining a degree.

As in Britain, certain universities are known for being stronger in certain subjects rather than in others, such as the Université Catholique de Louvain (UCL) which teaches medicine at the campus at the Hôpital St Luc, Woluwé,

Education for All Ages

and is strong in engineering at its main premises at Louvain-la-Neuve, not far from Wavre; and the Faculté St Louis, which provides the first cycle of a specialised law course, but does not offer the full curriculum (students attending this college must move to another establishment to complete their studies).

The best known art school in the country, which has a worldwide reputation, is the Ecole Nationale Supérieure des Arts Visuels de la Cambre, situated in the calm beauty of Brussels' Abbaye de la Cambre. Another famous institution is the modern dance and ballet school created by Maurice Béjart, known as the Mudra. Many foreign students come to study under this maestro.

Adult Education
Adults already holding a degree may like to take the opportunity of continuing their education by doing postgraduate studies at one of the Belgian universities. Most expatriates seem to prefer to attend lectures at the ULB where it is also possible to study French if you have some basic knowledge of the language. There are special summer courses organised in August, too – not only to learn a language – but you will need to have a good working knowledge of French to follow them.

There are other semi-official language centres in Brussels offering excellent French language lessons, as well as numerous private schools, and the addresses of a few of the most popular are given, along with the most important institutions mentioned already in this chapter, in Appendix I.

Most communes run language courses, along with other programmes. This is especially true of the Flemish communes around Brussels, which generally provide weekly Dutch classes. The French or Dutch lessons are usually designed with the foreigner in mind, rather than for Belgians. Invariably, there is a small enrolment fee and students must pay for their books. Apart from that, most communes charge nothing for the lessons.

There is only a limited range of full-time, higher education programmes in English available in Belgium, whether it is for a daytime or evening course. One of the few possibilities is the College of Europe in Bruges which offers a daytime course for law, economics and political science graduates in European studies. Locally, the University of Boston works together with the Vrije Universiteit Brussel and provides a Master of Science in Management course, as well as a Master of Science in Computer Information Systems, both of which lead to an American management degree. Tuition can be full- or part-time.

In addition, the British Open University has a representative in Brussels who arranges for a certain amount of tutor-counselling locally, depending on the course followed. The Open University provides a range of degree courses by correspondence.

Specifically About Luxembourg

Education is not so easy for English-speaking families in Luxembourg as it is in Belgium: there are only two schools offering instruction in their native tongue. These are the American International School of Luxembourg and the European School. Both institutions take children from the age of four years right through to the end of the secondary schooling. The cost of education at the American International School is a little lower than that at its Brussels equivalent. The European School, which was the first educational establishment to open, educates the children of officials working in the European institutions, and is free to employees' families. A few fee-paying children of non-EEC personnel are accepted when space permits.

Although both these schools take children from an early age, education in Luxembourg is compulsory only from six years of age. The school-leaving age is sixteen. Children stay at primary school until the age of eleven. After that, there are three branches they can move to: the *lycée*, which offers an academic career leading to university; the middle school, which teaches more practical subjects; or there is the *école complémentaire*, which provides a general secondary education.

Tuition starts in the Luxembourg dialect. German is the first language taught at school, with French being introduced into the programme in the second year of primary school. As the child progresses through the

Education for All Ages

educational system, French becomes increasingly more important until it completely replaces German as the language of instruction. English is taught in secondary school.

There is no university, but pupils gaining a diploma from the *lycée* can take a one-year course prior to entering a European university. Alternatively, they can apply to a foreign university for acceptance straight from the *lycée*.

The Miami University European Center, a branch of the American seat of learning in Oxford, Ohio, is situated in Luxembourg. It was founded to provide American students with a first-hand experience of Europe. American and Luxembourg professors teach courses in English, French and German language and literature, history, geography, economic and political sciences, art and drama to just over a hundred pupils annually. Students stay for a period of two semesters.

8
About Health and Health Services

If you arrive in Belgium in winter you may be given the impression that the whole nation is seriously ill as it is rare to hear anyone say that he has a cold: most infections start at 'flu (*la grippe*). Nor should you panic if your doctor says that one of your children is suffering from an '*angine*' when you thought that it was a very bad sore throat. It is just the vocabulary used here.

But Belgium does have a very well-organised, private health service to which everyone is obliged to contribute through national insurance payments. Anyone who has been paying regularly into the British health scheme and who joins the Belgian sickness insurance fund on arrival receives exactly the same coverage as Belgians. Americans can live and work in Belgium for five years before being obliged to contribute to Belgian social security. For the first five years they can contribute to either the Belgian or the US scheme; afterwards they must contribute either to both schemes or just to the Belgian one.

Many companies arrange additional medical insurance for their personnel which covers the difference between the amount reimbursed by the compulsory sickness fund and the real price. When the employer does not offer this extra coverage people often take out their own policies, especially in order to meet additional hospital expenses, such as for a private room.

The health scheme is operated by private mutualities or sickness funds. You may join whichever one you wish but it is more usual for foreigners to take the one used by the first employer since he will know more about the advantages offered and have the right contacts when you need to make a claim. The employee's contribution is deducted at source, as part of the national insurance contribution; independent workers have to make their own arrange-

About Health and Health Services

ments and their contributions are payable on a three-monthly basis. There is no ceiling to the amount that is deducted, both the employer's and the employee's payments being a percentage of the salary earned.

The mutuality provides a variety of services. It has a staff of doctors, dentists and other specialists that you may consult, although normally for the first visit, at least, you will not be able to make an appointment; it is generally only when you go back for treatment or special tests that an appointment will be made. Some mutualities have their own clinics where you can be hospitalised if the need arises. The rates for utilising your mutuality's services are generally lower than those charged by a doctor, dentist, specialist, hospital or clinic of your choice. In addition, there are mutualities that organise holidays for children and, sometimes, their mothers at very reasonable prices. You will probably be supplied with a brochure outlining the full advantages of membership on joining.

The disadvantage of using the mutuality's facilities is that they are never on your doorstep. Consequently, most expatriates prefer to go to a local physician. You are free to go to whichever practitioner you want and to go direct to a specialist, although your own doctor can refer you to one. Parents often go to a paediatrician with their children's illnesses although general practitioners are quite capable of dealing with common illnesses. The local physician will also be prepared to make house calls whereas the paediatrician is less likely to. In addition, each town or village has a centre to which children can be taken for free consultation. The town hall will be able to provide you with details of your nearest centre.

You will waste less time, but perhaps pay a little more, if you make an appointment with your doctor. Most physicians take patients by appointment, some exclusively. The term to use in French is a *rendez-vous*; the word *consultation* means a general surgery time when you go and wait your turn. (The Dutch equivalent for an appointment is an *afspraak*.) Doctors in major towns tend to see patients between 9am and about 8pm; in country areas physicians can receive patients from as early as 7.30am–9 or 10pm. It is usually possible to make an

About Health and Health Services

appointment to see a general practitioner within a day or two of calling. In cases where a patient is too ill to go out, most family physicians will visit at home. Each commune has its rota of doctors on call at weekends. Usually, if you dial your doctor's number, a message on his answering machine will indicate the weekend number to call. Otherwise, the local duty chemist will be able to tell you or it may be published in the local paper.

Generally speaking, physicians are very thorough. They will take blood pressure and pulse regularly and make other basic tests even for ordinary ailments. They are particularly aware of tropical diseases, diabetes, cancer and coronary ailments. A large number of by-pass operations are performed successfully each year, and the Bordet cancer clinic has a worldwide reputation, as has the tropical diseases hospital in Antwerp.

At the end of your consultation, your doctor will prescribe any medicine you need and will hand over the form to you. He will also expect to be paid or, in some cases, you should pay his receptionist for your visit. It is not usual to pay a physician by cheque since the amount is generally not very high. As a receipt, he will hand you a form which gives his details and a code relating in a very general way to the nature of the visit (consultation, surgery visit, tests, etc). To claim for reimbursement from your mutuality, you must complete the document and either send or take it to the fund's office, quoting your membership number. You will be reimbursed from between two-thirds and 75 per cent of the fee charged depending on whether you attended the surgery or made a special appointment with the doctor. You can ask for the money to be paid into a bank account, sent through the postal giro system, or paid cash if you present the documents in person. Some mutualities use a book system which needs to be sent or taken when making a claim.

The prescription has to be taken to a chemist, together with one of the stickers — which bear your name and membership number — sent to you in sheets by your mutuality. This will enable you to obtain the maximum reduction for the type of medicine prescribed. Medicines are coded with different letters to indicate the amount to

About Health and Health Services

be reimbursed: a large 'A' indicates that 100 per cent reimbursement is to be given; a 'B' indicates 75 per cent will be reimbursed; a 'C' means that 50 per cent of the cost will be returned; a 'Cs' means that you will get back only 40 per cent; and 'D' category does not qualify for any reimbursement. (The contraceptive pill comes under the 'D' category.)

Chemists open at the same times as other shops, and are sometimes closed over lunchtime. They are open five days a week but there is always one on duty at the weekend. Your local chemist, if it is not his turn, will display the address of the duty chemist for that weekend. Medicines purchased out of normal opening hours are subject to a small surcharge.

If there is something wrong with you that your own physician is unable to handle he will suggest that you see a specialist. He will probably recommend one of whom he has specific knowledge; however, you are not obliged to go to that person and you can ask to see someone else. Your doctor will give you a letter to take to the specialist and, normally, you ring through to make an appointment. Should you need to receive treatment or to be operated on in hospital, you will have to go to the one where the specialist is practising.

Unless you are taken in as an emergency case, the hospital will send you a letter giving you a date and time for entry. You will be expected to pay a deposit at the latest by the time you have checked in – and this goes for emergency patients, too. Some hospitals will arrange with your mutuality to obtain payment direct for its part; others will expect you to pay the full bill and then to contact your mutuality in the usual way for reimbursement.

Hospitals vary as much as at home in that some are extremely modern and like a first-class hotel, while others are older and not so well equipped. In most you will have the opportunity of sharing a room with two or more people or having a room on your own. Prices will vary accordingly.

One important point to remember when telephoning or visiting a married woman in hospital is to ask for her by her maiden name as she will appear on hospital records by

About Health and Health Services

that name only. For the same reason, many well-meaning bouquets of flowers go astray.

A pregnant woman will usually make regular visits either to her family physician or to a gynaecologist. About six months into the pregnancy she will register with the hospital where her baby will be born. If you consult a gynaecologist and wish to have your baby in a specific hospital, you should make sure that the gynaecologist you choose is practising there.

Antenatal exercises can be arranged privately with a kinesitherapist. They can be also done at the hospital where courses involve about one hour's exercise per week, learning about the baby's development and how to prepare for its birth as well. Some hospitals provide evening lectures on different subjects pertaining to the new-born baby's care. During the last session and prior to going in for the birth, the mother will probably be taken around the various sections of the maternity unit to familiarise her with the procedure. It is likely that the kinesitherapist who has taken the courses which the mother has been attending will be present at the birth to help her during her contractions. Immediately the baby is born it will be looked after by a paediatrician, not a nurse, and this will continue as long as it is in hospital.

Post-natal exercises will be begun in the hospital and can be continued privately after the mother has returned home or she can attend further courses at the hospital. From about the third week she will attend a weekly post-natal clinic which can last for as long as three months. Post-natal follow-up is assured by the hospital, family physician or the paeditrician.

The mother also has the opportunity of taking the baby to the local paediatric clinic until the child is six years old. From birth until the age of three, the visits take place on a monthly basis; from three years they become three-monthly. Each child has its own book in which details of its weight, measurements and any medical history are recorded.

A visit to a dentist is very similar to a visit to the doctor. However, it is far more usual to make an appointment when going to the dentist and you may have to wait several weeks to be seen. If you are in pain, though, a

About Health and Health Services

dentist will normally fit you in when there is a cancellation. Not all dentists will match fillings that are likely to show to the colour of your teeth. You will have to ask to have this done. Gold fillings are popular – and expensive. Dentists are usually very attentive to children's teeth and will take corrective action with any problem from as early an age as possible. Most dental surgeries have very modern equipment.

You will receive a similar form from the dentist on paying for your treatment as you receive from the doctor and this, too, should be submitted to your mutuality for reimbursement.

Normal health insurance does not cover all aspects of medicine. For example, if you attend a physiotherapist, without having been sent by a physician, you will not be reimbursed any of the cost. Also, not every osteopath or practitioner of acupuncture will be recognised by the mutualities and so it is wise to check first if you will be reimbursed part of the cost of treatment. The assistance of a nurse, for such tasks as administering injections or taking care of anyone who is bedridden, is another area where you cannot make a claim to the mutuality. However, there are private organisations, such as the Croix Jaune et Blanc, that, for an annual subscription of the equivalent of a few pounds a year for the whole family, will provide such a service.

Ambulances are operated privately in Belgium; however, the twenty-four hour emergency service (contacted by dialling 900) will rush a patient to the nearest hospital best equipped to deal with the crisis of the moment.

Most people prefer to speak their own language when dealing with health problems. This presents no real difficulty in Belgium since a large number of the medical books that student doctors and dentists have had to read – and many of those they continue to consult – are in English. However, if you want to be sure that your doctor really does speak English well enough to understand your problems, there are several lists of English-speaking medical practitioners available: from your embassy, from the British & Commonwealth Women's Club and the American Women's Club, and from some of the schools' parent-teacher associations.

About Health and Health Services

Specifically About Luxembourg

While the medical service in Luxembourg is very similar to that in Belgium, the telephone number to dial in an emergency is different. In Luxembourg, 012 covers not only the ambulance but all the emergency services including those of the police, gendarmerie, fire department and locksmiths. The person replying can also tell you the numbers to contact for the duty chemists and hospitals, since not all hospitals in the Grand Duchy provide twenty-four hour casualty services.

9
Day-to-Day Living

Getting to know people in the hope of forming friendships is one of the most difficult parts of moving to a new country. Anyone working will automatically come into contact with people who could be potential friends, just as children will find new chums at school. Women at home, however, often find it more difficult.

Most women will find it a help in getting to know their way around if they take out membership in their nationality's women's club. The British and Commonwealth Women's Club (BCWC), as the name indicates, is open to more than one nationality and is for women of all ages, married or single. As one of the committee members remarked recently, 'most of us involved in running the club are not what is generally termed the "clubby" type but the BCWC keeps us active and provides a useful service for those who need its support'.

The clubhouse adjoins the Madison sports club in Auderghem, a pleasant suburb of Brussels. Although the address is Luxor Park, it is reached by either the Avenue Nénuphars, the Avenue Génicot or the Avenue Tedesco – and not the Rue Luxor Park – and then by following an old railway siding until you arrive in the sports club's car park, which the BCWC uses, too. The situation sounds unusual and isolated, which it is, but the clubhouse, once you reach it, has lots of character and something very English about it, even before you step inside. It is in delightful surroundings, set in a private park with tennis courts that are available for members' use. The premises consist of a lounge and restaurant-cum-bar area, a library, two small meetings rooms, a pleasant kitchen, and a small office. It is open daily in the week, except during major holiday periods, and light lunches are served at midday. Members can take friends in and the library is open to husbands and children. There is almost unlimited parking, and access by public transport is good although there is a fair walk from the bus stop or metro station.

The BCWC has over six hundred members who meet together, regularly or irregularly, for a wide variety of activities in the clubhouse or in the area in which they live. Each person is attached to one of the eleven areas which are often small clubs within the main club and are invaluable to newcomers needing advice and information on such things as schools, shops and local services. Most areas hold regular coffee mornings in members' homes; sometimes there is a specific aim in view, such as fundraising, but they all help to introduce new members to their nearest BCWC neighbours. Each area has its own hostess and she is responsible for welcoming and helping each new member to integrate in her area. Three areas, Overijse, Waterloo and Tervuren, have their own libraries, in addition to the central clubhouse collection, which contains over four thousand books, with about ten new volumes being added each month.

A magazine, *Passport*, produced by the members, is published ten times a year, which keeps members informed of activities and events, and the larger areas produce their own local information sheet which is delivered to members in that district.

The young wives' group of the club aims to help the needs of young mothers in particular. It arranges special play afternoons and outings for the children, as well as activities for the wives themselves.

However, when you first join the club, whatever your age, you will find you are made especially welcome at the 'open house' events and clubhouse coffee mornings.

Club activities cover a wide range of interests. There are special classes for everything from art to Indian cookery, from badminton to bodyworks exercises and from bridge to languages (French and German), with outside groups that follow their particular interests, such as the lunch club which samples the delights of local restaurants and another group which makes museum visits.

Not all of the activities take place in the daytime or during the week so that single people and husbands, and

Day-to-Day Living

sometimes the whole family, can join in from time to time. A wine-tasting will be held in the evening and a 'beetle drive' or supper dance on a Saturday night. Additional events added to the programme in 1985 included a ball at the Château de la Hulpe, a Laura Ashley fashion show and a midsummer musical gala at the Château du Lac, Genval.

American women have their own club, too. The largest of the national foreign women's clubs, it is housed in a delightful villa at Rhode-St-Genèse, close to the Fôret de Soignes. Non-American wives may be eligible for membership of that club, too, particularly if their husbands work for an American company. This could be especially convenient if you plan to live out in the region of Waterloo or beyond. The American Women's Club premises comprise several activities rooms, a restaurant, crêche, gymnasium, library and several outdoor tennis courts.

The enormous list of activities available to members at the beginning of 1986 was divided into '*chez-vous*', cultural, language and sports, games and health categories. In '*chez-vous*' classes were offered everything from Cajun cookin' to first-aid for tots. The cultural activities represented varied from Brussels by foot in April to Chinese philosophy (Taoism). The language classes allow the study of French at all levels as well as basic Dutch. In the sports, games and health section an alpine fitness week was scheduled, as well as instruction on cardiopulmonary resuscitation, and horseback riding.

The American Women's Club is also particularly active in organising special trips to places of interest in Belgium and abroad. These vary from a one-day excursion for members to several days when the whole family can join in as well.

The club has its own magazine, *Rendez-vous*, which keeps members informed of forthcoming events and relevant news.

Other nationalities, such as the Canadians, have their women's clubs, too. The Canadian club is not only open to all women of that nationality, but also to those married to Canadians or those having resided in Canada for ten years. It holds craft classes, group discussions, arranges tours, family and evening gatherings.

For those who would like to meet women of different nationalities, there are several clubs that provide such an opportunity. One is the Women's International Club, which is not as orientated towards the newcomer as the three already mentioned since its main objective is to bring different nationalities together. For that reason, it limits its membership of any one nationality to a fixed percentage of the total in order to keep a good balance.

There are women's groups that meet together for specific interests, such as the International Women's Register which has grown out of the Housewives' Register. It gives house-bound women a chance to get together with others in the same situation and to discuss a wide range of topics. Members are given research projects and report on their findings at a meeting when the subject is debated in some detail. At the time of writing there are two such groups in Belgium: one in Brussels and the other in Wavre.

Pregnant women or mothers of young children are often concerned about what they can expect in the way of local pre- and post-natal care and support, and there are three clubs that offer advice in this important field. The National Childbirth Trust in Brussels aims at preparing for parenthood future mothers who are away from home and offers a comprehensive advisory service for mothers and fathers. It holds information meetings on childbirth, pre-natal classes, gives feeding advice and provides opportunities for mothers with babies to meet together and to exchange ideas. The La Lèche League Brussels is specifically involved in providing information and advice for mothers who wish to breast-feed their babies. On a more social level, the Mother & Baby Club helps young mothers to meet each other, to discuss common difficulties and to share their experiences.

The Women's Organisation for Equality (WOE) holds regular meetings on subjects of interest to its members at its premises in the Rue Blanche, which is just off the Avenue Louise. Another, newer organisation, Women for Peace, arranges weekly meetings for those supporting its cause.

Day-to-Day Living

Churches
Just as in our homelands, a number of activities here are centred around the local churches and all the main English-speaking Christian denominations have at least one place of worship in the country. Some, like the congregation of All Saints', Waterloo (really situated at Argenteuil), have a women's association. But there are a couple of interdenominational women's groups that meet regularly for social contact: the International Christian Women's Club and the Women's Aglow Christian Fellowship.

As for the denominations represented in the English-speaking community, you will find all the principal ones established here. All Saints is one of the joint Anglican (that is, Church of England) and American Episcopal churches of which the Brussels pro-cathedral of the Holy Trinity is the most important. Other Anglican churches in the country are situated in Antwerp, Ghent and Ostend with services also being held from time to time in Bruges, Charleroi, Knokke, Liège and Ypres.

Belgium is a predominantly Roman Catholic country although only a relatively small part of the population is practising. Therefore, foreigners who are Roman Catholics are well served as long as they can follow a mass in French or in Dutch. However, there are English-speaking Roman Catholic communities with their own services.

Other long-established and active communities in Belgium are those of the Church of Scotland, which meets at St Andrew's, just off the Avenue Louise, and the American Protestant Church, which holds regular services on the International School of Brussels campus. Attached to the International Baptist Church is a Women's Bible Fellowship.

Other religions that are represented in Brussels include the Assembly of God, the Baptists, the Christian Scientists, the American Lutheran Church, the Jews, the Quakers and the Mormons.

General Clubs
Since the British and the American communities have been established for a considerable time and neither is

small, there are plenty of clubs, covering a wide range of activities, ready to help you pass your leisure time. Many will be only too glad to find someone with a little time on their hands who can offer some assistance on the organisational side. The sort of work you are likely to be roped in for is giving a hand with mailing lists and publicity, taking bookings for amateur productions, making and adapting costumes, and even painting scenery and clubhouse premises.

Those interested in amateur dramatics will find some first-rate clubs putting on highly professional productions three or four times a year in local theatres. Whether you have a star part, work backstage, sell programmes on the night or support the effort from the stalls, your membership will always be appreciated. The English Comedy Club is the oldest of the dramatic societies and stages productions in period costume and modern dress. There is a traditional pantomime in early January. The American Theatre Company has recently introduced café theatres to its programme, in addition to the conventional productions. As would be expected, the Brussels Shakespeare Society promotes the Bard's works. There is also an active Irish Theatre Group bringing some of that country's writings to the notice of the Belgians, as well as the foreign community.

If you sing as well as act you will certainly find a welcome at the Brussels Gilbert and Sullivan Society which stages a production or two each year by those masters of light opera. Other choral groups, apart from church and women's club choirs, range from the Brussels Choral Society, which requires a voice test for entry, to the Society for Suppressed Songsters, where anyone who feels like opening their mouth and emitting a sound can join in. The second of these two clubs holds a traditional Christmas carol concert in one of the biggest auditoriums in the capital each December and puts on fun evenings such as the 'Messiah from Scratch' with similar popularity.

There are very few restaurants where you can dine and dance and, fortunately, many of the long-established clubs hold dinner-dances at least once a year. However, for those who like dancing there are one or two clubs to join.

Day-to-Day Living

Mannekens 'n Maids is a square-dancing group and Swing Partners holds fairly regular barn dances at which there is folk and square dancing. The Caledonian Society holds weekly sessions of Scottish dancing, but is also in existence to keep alive and promote Scottish traditions in general. Consequently, it organises piping classes and holds Highland games every summer. The club has special celebration dinners for Burns Night, St Andrew's Day and Hogmanay.

The Brussels British Community Association (BBCA) is probably the largest of the national clubs, acting as an umbrella organisation for twenty-five constituent groups. The BBCA is also responsible for the Queen's Birthday Reception at the Ambassador's Residence and an annual sports day for members' children. The Wales in Europe Group, which has a small membership owing to the low number of that nationality residing in Belgium, also welcomes the non-Welsh to attend its gatherings. The American Club of Brussels, which has an office in the Brussels Sheraton Hotel, holds a monthly final-Friday cocktail party, organises luncheons and the annual Fourth of July celebration weekend. There is an active Irish Club as well.

Sports rank high in community activities and expatriate clubs exist for football, badminton, rugby, broomball, darts, squash and cricket. Those which have made a specific place for themselves in the local sporting programme include the Royal Brussels British Football Club which plays at Werchter near Haecht, the Brussels United Football Club, which has two teams in the Belgian Amateur Soccer League and whose home ground is in Perk, and the Brussels British Rugby Club, which also runs two sides in the Belgian League championship and which plays at Wolvertem, north of Brussels. Whilst the word 'British' often appears in the title of the long-established clubs, it is rare for any nationality restrictions to be put on membership, and players invariably represent as wide a variety of countries as those newer clubs in whose title there is no reference to nationality.

For youngsters, the EuroBrit United Football Club, which plays at the British School of Brussels, aims to provide soccer for boys of expatriate families living in the

Brussels area. It is multinational and comprises five age groups ranging from the pre-minims, who are under ten years old, to the juniors, aged between sixteen and twenty. A second club, the Brussels Sports Association, organises an annual soccer programme for children between six and fourteen, meeting at the International School of Brussels.

Business people have their clubs, too. There are British and American Chambers of Commerce, as well as a Canadian Businessmen's Club, a European Business Group in Belgium, the European Association of Professional Secretaries and the Toastmasters Club of Brussels. Other groups, such as the Belgo-British Union, the English-Speaking Union of Belgium and the American-Belgian Association, promote ties between their own country and that of the host nation.

There are clubs for people having gone through similar experiences: the Royal Air Force Association, the Royal British Legion, the Royal Naval Association, and SPA (Single Parents Association). Political clubs are not lacking either, and such groups as the British Conservative Association in Belgium, British Labour Group, Brussels area party of the UK Social Democratic Party, US Democrats Abroad and US Republicans Abroad are all active in their various ways, as are certain pressure groups, such as ARBA (the Association for the Rights of Britons Abroad) and the Joint Task Force on Development Issues.

Children will find that there are plenty of activities for them, too. In fact, some mothers find themselves doing nothing but ferrying their children from one place to another after school hours. There are local cub, brownie, scouts, guide and venture groups which meet on a regular basis. Both the BBCA and the BCWC actively support the British scouting movement and will provide details of whom to contact for the names of the current leaders. The scouting association does sometimes give notification of its activities through *The Bulletin* and *The Belgian Weekly Gazette*, but not very often since most packs have waiting lists for membership; a number are listed in *Living in Belgium & Luxembourg*. The American scouting movement, whether it is for boys or girls, is generally organised through the schools and details can be obtained from them. For instance, the Cub Scout Pack 194

Day-to-Day Living

meets at the International School of Brussels, but boys do not have to attend the ISB to join.

For those who want to help others by becoming involved with charity work there is much to do. The British Charitable Fund, of which King Baudouin is the patron, was founded in 1815 by the Duke of Wellington after the Battle of Waterloo and continues to provide assistance to needy persons of British nationality and their spouses living in Belgium. You will be surprised to find how many elderly people with British connections this organisation has on its list today: people who came to Belgium, sometimes during World War I, married and stayed on.

The Community Help Service (CHS) is another organisation which would welcome voluntary assistance. Probably the most noticeable service it provides is the Help Line (02/648 40 14) which is operated on a twenty-four hour basis and is essentially a crisis and information telephone service staffed by trained volunteers. The office is open weekdays to deal with all the problems associated with culture shock: children's learning difficulties, parenting problems, drug and alcohol addiction, depression, acute distress and behavioural change, and marital and family difficulties. The professional staff is available for consultation outside these hours by appointment. The therapists do charge for their services where those receiving help can pay for it, but the CHS, as such, does not pay any professional salaries. Administrative costs are met by donations from private individuals and company contributions as well as from special fund-raising efforts, such as the Yellow Umbrella second-hand clothes shops, situated on the mezzanine floor in the Galerie Rivoli at the Bascule, and the second-hand bookshop near Woluwé Shopping Centre.

Some years ago, the United Fund of Belgium was set up by a group of expatriate businessmen as a way of attracting donations from the foreign business community and distributing them to worthy charitable projects in Belgium. It is run by a team of voluntary expatriate fund-raisers and an independent allocations committee which is composed entirely of Belgian nationals. Financial help goes to everything from combating sudden death syndrome in infants to special baths

Antwerp, Belgium's second largest city and one of Europe's biggest ports, is often neglected by tourists, yet it contains some of the country's most important museums and monuments. It also has considerable charm, not always associated with harbour cities. Alleys such as this provide short cuts between side streets off the famous Meir (*Belgian National Tourist Office*)

Best-known of all the Belgian carnivals, that of Binche in Wallonia attracts large crowds on the three days preceding Ash Wednesday. But the preparations start weeks before and every stage is significant, culminating in the Shrove Tuesday parade when the *Gille*s don their magnificent ostrich-plumed head-dresses and dance their way around the town (*Belgian National Tourist Office*)

to ease the lives of the severely handicapped.

Another initiative of the expatriate community is the introduction of the hospice movement, previously unknown in Belgium. Continuing Care Community, as it is known here, has just set up a home care unit which provides specialised care for the dying. It can now provide care for patients for whom active medical treatment no longer provides any prospect of cure. The care includes conventional medical treatment, but places a special emphasis on nursing care, the control of pain, and the emotional and spiritual needs of both patient and family. The community needs both professional and non-professional helpers in the unit and in making its object known and raising funds.

Many people coming to Belgium will be glad to know that there are some very good English libraries in Brussels. We have already mentioned those of the two largest women's clubs, but there is also the British Council Library, which contains some fourteen thousand books, and the American Library. Both are lending and reference libraries. In addition, there is a large Children's Library.

Other clubs exist to introduce people of different nationalities to each other. One example is People to People which organises a variety of social events for its members. Another is the Cercle Polyglotte de Bruxelles which holds conversation evenings once a week when members are able to practise foreign languages.

Community Activities in Antwerp

There are two women's clubs in the Antwerp district: the Antwerp British Women's Association and the American Women's Club, both of which meet once a month and have types of activities similar to their Brussels counterparts but on a smaller scale. There is also a branch of the International Women's Register in the city.

As far as churches are concerned, there is an Anglican church, St Boniface, which holds regular services. St Boniface has a playgroup, too, which meets one afternoon a week in the church hall, the same place as for the Brownies. The American Protestant Church of Antwerp holds its services in the Swedish Seamen's Chapel, and an

Day-to-Day Living

English-language Roman Catholic mass is said in the Heilig Hart Instituut.

The Antwerp British Community Association is the general social organisation of the British, whilst American men have their own club which meets at the American Belgian Association clubhouse. Similarly, there is a Royal British Belgian Association promoting British and Belgian relations.

Drama in Antwerp is provided by the British American Theatrical Society which produces four full productions a year, including a pantomime. There is also a cricket club and a Common Market Squash Club. Antwerp, like several cities in Belgium, has its own branch of the Royal British Legion.

A branch of the American girl scouts meets at the Antwerp International School.

The clubs mentioned in this chapter that have no official base generally announce their activities in the 'Happenings' section of *The Bulletin* or in *The Belgian Weekly Gazette*. A contact name and telephone number is given, too, in the 'Directory' sections of the current issue of *Living in Belgium & Luxembourg*. The full addresses of the various denominations named are listed in Appendix 1 (page 180–3).

Entertainment

Belgium has much to offer in the way of entertainment if you take the trouble to go and look for it. For example, there are some extremely good operatic productions, starring internationally acclaimed singers, staged in Brussels, usually at the Théâtre de la Monnaie or the Cirque Royal. On the whole, the classics are performed, although some modern works do get aired, particularly in the smaller hall of the Monnaie. Belgium is perhaps better known abroad for its Twentieth Century Ballet (*Ballet du 20ième Siècle*), founded and directed by Maurice Béjart. Members of this troupe usually provide any ballets required in operas produced by the Monnaie, in addition to their own scheduled ballet programmes.

Theatre is generally in French or Dutch although, from time to time, English-language productions are performed by touring companies which visit Belgium, mostly under the sponsorship of the British Council or with the help of the American Embassy cultural department.

Marionettes provide another kind of theatre that is highly developed as an art form. The most famous troupe is Toone which acts out satirical versions of famous works (like *Hamlet*, the *St Matthew Passion*, and *Macbeth*) with rod puppets in a minute theatre where the audience sits on badly but gaily padded wooden benches. The works, even if they are enacted in a sort of period costume, are remarkably up-to-date, poking fun at anyone currently in the local news. The words are spoken by one person, Toone, the traditional name of the master puppeteer, and are in the Brussels dialect, a mixture of French and Flemish. The incredible thing is that no matter how little French you understand, the atmosphere of the show will convey enough for you to enjoy it.

Belgium is particularly rich in musical activities serving a wide variety of tastes and featuring important national and international musicians. The late Queen Elisabeth founded a major annual musical competition which, over three years, alternates between piano, violin and composition. Out of ten or so finalists each year, there are few who are not launched instantaneously on the path to international fame. In addition to this competition, held in the month of May, there are three major festivals, two of them annual and solely musical by nature, and the third taking place every two years which includes art exhibitions and theatre. The first two are known as the Festival of Flanders and the Festival of Wallonia and cover several months and several cities in their respective parts of the country.

For those who work in the city some midday concerts are organised, with those in the series *Concerts du Midi* taking place on a regular basis.

The *BBB Agenda* guide provides a complete programme of all the cultural events taking place in the Brussels area during the week. It is produced by the Brussels city tourist office, which is housed in the Hôtel de Ville, and which also provides a theatre, concert and opera booking service, Teletib, for subscribers. This is an excellent way of making sure that you obtain seats for the productions you want to attend.

Day-to-Day Living

There are some superb art exhibitions mounted, especially at the Palais des Beaux-Arts and the Modern Art Museum.

Cinema-buffs need not fear that they are going to miss seeing the latest movies. In fact, Brussels receives most of the good British and American ones very quickly after their release and they are always shown in the original version in the centre of the city, with French and Dutch sub-titles. It is only in the suburbs and in small towns that films are shown dubbed. Lovers of the classical movies will soon find their way to the cinema museum (Musée du Cinéma) which shows five old movies a day. It is housed in part of the Palais des Beaux-Arts and membership, which is very cheap, will entitle you to receive the monthly programme by post. At most cinemas there are usually special children's programmes on Wednesday afternoons.

And if you prefer to sit at home and watch a film, you will find plenty of choice on the numerous television stations available on the cable. In the Brussels area, you will certainly be able to pick up the following television stations: two French-speaking (RTBF) and two Dutch-speaking (BRT) Belgian, two BBC, two Dutch, three French, three German and one Luxembourg (RTL). You may also capture the Italian station (RAI) and TV5, a multinational, French-speaking channel. It is usually only on the Dutch-language stations (that is, BRT and the Dutch ones) that you will find English films being shown in English with French and Dutch sub-titles; the other stations generally show translated versions. Dutch-language stations show a lot of British and American television programmes.

You can receive BBC radio, although it will probably only be Radio 2 and the World Service unless you have a very powerful set; Americans can pick up the AFN (American Forces Network) transmission which is primarily designed for SHAPE.

Specifically About Luxembourg

Both the British Ladies' Club and the American Women's Club, if much smaller than their Belgian counterparts, are very active in organising meetings and events of

Day-to-Day Living

interest to their members. Neither has a clubhouse but the telephone number of the current person to contact is published from time to time in the *Luxembourg News Digest* or in the latest edition of *Living in Luxembourg & Belgium*. Both clubs have a monthly newsletter which is sent to members. Other women's organisations for English-speaking people include a branch of the La Lèche League and Weightwatchers Club.

Business people have the British Businessmen's Luncheon Club and the Bossuet Gavaliers Toastmaster Club. Political groups meeting to further their causes are the Left Club of Luxembourg and the Social Democratic Party (UK). In the pressure group section the Association for the Rights of Britons Abroad is represented here, as is the Action Aid Support Group, which works to raise funds for self-help projects in Africa and India. On the more general social scene there is the International Friendship Club, American–Luxembourg Society, and the Irish Club of Luxembourg. These is also a branch of the Royal Air Forces Association.

Amateur dramatics flourish, too, and are of a high standard. Dionysus Theatricals, the New World Theatre Club and Pirate Products, the latter specialising in light opera, all make regular contributions to local cultural activities.

If you are a keen sportsperson, Luxembourg has its own cricket, darts, squash, rugby, and men's and ladies' hockey clubs. Those who like horse-riding will find plenty of stables although some provide livery only. Skating and curling are both available in this country that generally has a ruder winter than Belgium.

Several clubs organise activities for children, too, but, in addition there are Telstar Scouts for boys from seven to sixteen years old and Troop 310 which meets at the American International School.

English-speaking churches exist for the Anglican Episcopal community, for Roman Catholics, for those of the Evangelical faith, for Mormons, and the Quakers hold regular meetings.

For those who like reading there is the British Library and the Miami University Library, both in Luxembourg city. They are not necessarily open all day and every day so

Day-to-Day Living

it is wise to telephone first to save a disappointing journey.

Luxembourg has two main theatres, the Théâtre Municipal and the new Théâtre des Capucins, where concerts, plays and sometimes ballet and opera are staged. There is a very good quarterly calendar of events, *Vade-Mecum Culturel*, which is issued by the city tourist office and which lists all forthcoming events at these theatres and at the music conservatory, as well as at art galleries and other cultural centres.

In the summer there are regular concerts held in the shady Place d'Armes, in front of the city tourist office. There is also a music festival featuring classical and popular artists of international reputation which takes place about the same time of year in the pretty town of Echternach.

Many British and American films are shown in Luxembourg city and they are generally in their original version.

BBC television has not yet come to Luxembourg. The stations received are the French and German RTL channels and, with the cable, those of the surrounding countries: Belgium, France, and Germany. The RTL also puts out a community radio programme in English in the afternoons from Monday through Saturday. AFN and the BBC's World Service can also be received.

10
Eating and Drinking, and Shopping

When it comes to entertainment, most Belgians would probably not consider eating as their favourite activity because it is an essential of life. However, it is virtually a national pastime to be enjoyed and to be taken very seriously. Hours are spent at the table sampling one local speciality after another — and Belgian cuisine produces much that is worthy of being sampled by the best gastronomes. Many a Frenchman has admitted that Belgian cuisine is, on the whole, better than that of France in that the standard of its excellence is consistently high.

Before you go off in search of the local pizzeria or Indian eating house — which will be just as highly priced as a comparable or even lesser Belgian establishment — do try some local cooking. The 'menu' generally represents good value for money and you have the advantage of knowing exactly what the end price will be. (VAT and service are included in the price on Belgian restaurant cards.) At lunchtime, in ordinary restaurants, there will be a menu of the day (*menu du jour*) or, perhaps, simply a dish of the day (*plat du jour*), the difference being that the first will contain at least two courses while the second is just one dish. The 'menu' or '*plat du jour*' offers the advantage that it will have been prepared fresh that day and will have been cooked in sufficient quantity so that you can be served almost immediately.

Even in Belgium's many top quality restaurants you will invariably find a 'menu' as well as the *à la carte* dishes to choose from. The '*menu de dégustation*' will feature the chef's specialties and show off his culinary expertise at its best. It may come under the guise of some other title, such as a seasonal menu (*menu de saison*).

There are certain main eating areas in and around

Eating and Drinking, and Shopping

Brussels but that does not mean to say that all the restaurants there are good, nor does it mean that the area is a tourist trap. There will be certain time-honoured establishments which have an excellent reputation and where you will be given value for money. They will not necessarily be the most expensive or the most showy in the area, either. But the fact that they have survived so long means that they have a faithful clientele. It is the others round about, that have grown up because of that reputation and, perhaps, because of the attractiveness of the neighbourhood, that are the tourist traps.

Three such areas that come immediately to mind are the Place Ste Catherine which, due to its historical position as the fish market, is surrounded by fish restaurants; the Ilôt Sacré, the very old area through which the Rue des Bouchers passes; and the Grand Sablon, another picturesque square in the antiques dealers' quarter. A village popular with the people of Brussels on a fine Sunday lunchtime is the hamlet of Jezus-Eik (Notre-Dame-au-Bois in the extremely loose French translation; the correct, Flemish name means Jesus's oak), on the edge of the Forêt de Soignes and full of restaurants, many of which have terraces where you can eat outdoors in reasonable weather.

If you are looking for a guarantee that you will eat well you could not do better than to make a reservation at one of the thirty-three establishments that have been invited to join the *Ordre des 33 Maîtres-Queux de Belgique*. Founded in the early 1960s, all the establishments have to be owned by their chefs. Among the order's objectives is the promotion of Belgian cuisine and local products throughout Europe, although this has not deterred them from taking their art to places as far away as China. While some of these restaurants have accommodation as well, another association, the '*Etapes de Bon Goût*', ensures good food and a comfortable hotel.

At the coast, fish is predominant on the menu as well as in certain restaurants in Brussels and elsewhere. I have met many British people who detested fish until they came to Belgium because they had never had the opportunity to experience really fresh fish such as is to be found here. Mussels are a great delicacy and are served prepared in numerous ways although the most common is *moules marinières* (steamed with vegetables and a glass of white wine, which provide the base for a creamy sauce). Oysters, too, are popular although it is difficult to find the creamy Butley variety from Orford.

In the autumn, restaurants in the Ardennes often have a special game menu, one of the highlights of Belgium's gastronomic pleasures. Apart from the more commonplace pheasant and hare, you will be offered various types of venison (*biche, faon,* and *chevreuil*), wild boar (*sanglier*) and its young (*marcassin*), partridge (*perdrix*), woodcock (*bécasse*) and quail (*caille*).

Some of the best known specialties of the Belgian cuisine are: *jambon d'Ardennes,* a strongly flavoured smoked ham; *tomate aux crevettes,* tomato stuffed with shrimps; *fondus,* small squares of breaded cheese that have been deep-fried; *escavêche,* mixed fish cooked in vinegar and served cold in its jelly; *carbonnades flamandes,* a tasty beef stew cooked in a special local beer called gueuze; *waterzooi,* which is mostly made with chicken today – but originated from Ghent where fish was the main ingredient – served in a creamy sauce made with fresh vegetables; *faisan à la Brabançonne,* pheasant braised together with chicory; *lapin aux pruneaux,* rabbit cooked with prunes; *oie à l'Instar de Visé,* a preparation of goose; *rognons de veau à la liégeoise,* veal kidneys sautéed with juniper berries; *tarte au sucre,* a delicious gooey affair; *tarte au riz,* a rice tart; *tarte au matton,* a tart with a cheese-curd filling; *tarte à l'Djotte,* a specialty from Nivelles made with cheese and herbs; *pain d'épice,* a sweet spicy cake; *speculoos,* a special biscuit normally served with coffee and, at St Nicholas-tide, made into large figures of the saint for children; *gauffres,* a waffle served with icing-sugar, whipped cream or fruit.

Of the many gastronomic ingredients produced in the country and which figure so predominantly in the Belgian cuisine – strawberries, hop shoots, white asparagus, red cabbage, chervil, crayfish, leeks and wild boar – chicory is worth singling out because its culinary uses were discovered in this country over a century ago. Some farmers' wives at Evere, near to Brussels, found that the chicory roots, stocked for sale to producers of the drink,

Eating and Drinking, and Shopping

grew new leaves like a tulip bulb in the dark during winter. Experimenting with the growth, they discovered that it could be eaten as a salad or cooked and served as a vegetable. Locally, it is called *witloof* in the original Flemish, or *chicon* in French. In the States and in France it is known as Belgian endive.

One of the few complaints Britons often have about the average Belgian restaurant is that no vegetable, other than potato, is served with the main course. This is probably due to the fact that vegetables are very expensive and, also, because Belgians like a good soup to start their meal and these are mostly vegetable-based. If you eat in a Belgian home, however, you will find that most households eat two vegetables.

Like Britain, Belgium has been adding recently to its variety of locally produced cheeses. The range now covers the cream cheeses, like the slightly lumpy *maquée* from the Walloon region and the more common *Petits Suisses*, the soft, fermented cheeses such as the strong *Boulette de Huy* and the *Herve*, the semi-hard fermented cheeses like the Maredsous, Lo and the Passendael, and the hard cheeses like the *broodkaas*. Certain have been developed in abbeys together with a special beer, such as Maredsous and Lo/St Sixtus, and these are best savoured with the local beverage. The soft white cheese of Brabant should be eaten spread lavishly on an enormous slice of dark brown bread, garnished with spring onions and radishes and washed down with a 'kriek' (a cherry-based beer) or a gueuze.

Wine has become more popular as an accompaniment to the meal than the traditional beverage, beer. Belgium has no real wine production of its own to speak of although the growers of the hot-house grapes in the Hoeilaart/Overijse region close to Brussels have tried, not very successfully. Now, the country that was once high up in the scale of beer consumption, is dropping in its placing each year. It still manufactures over 400 different sorts of beer, however, at some 129 breweries and lovers of real ale will find their time well occupied sampling the Trappist and abbey beers, the regional brews and the specialty drinks such as kriek.

In general, Belgians are extremely quality conscious and

Eating and Drinking, and Shopping

food is no exception to the rule. In fact, it can be said that they buy with their eyes. Shop windows are extremely well decorated and make shopping a delight. The presentation is so important that when it comes to buying fruit or vegetables they will probably not be ripe or even nearly ripe when presented for purchase.

Rules are not so strict as they are in Britain on marking the origin and contents of foodstuffs. Such changes will come, if only as a result of the Common Market. However, certain restrictions have been put on the description of some meat products such as hamburgers, minced meat and sausages, and there is a move towards quality control on certain local specialities. (Ardennes ham is already subject to specific requirements).

Bread sold by a baker, rather than by a supermarket, is invariably baked on the premises and of a much better quality than most baker's bread in Britain. Cake shops abound and offer a tempting selection of cakes and often loose chocolates as well. Some bakers will have a tea room attached or at the back of the shop where you can indulge in a coffee and *croissant* in the morning or tea and a *gâteau* in the afternoon. It is quite common to find a bakery selling cakes and a cake shop selling bread, but it is rare for both items to be outstandingly good; normally, a shop will be stronger on bread or on cakes.

There is often much variety in the types of bread offered, and even *croissants* can be filled with chocolate or an almond mixture in addition to the regular kind. The choice of small and large cakes merits working your way steadily through the whole gamut. You will notice the considerable use of fresh cream. Tarts are another speciality with seasonal fruits figuring high in popularity; rice tart and cheese tart are also favourites.

Many bakers will deliver and, in city centres, it is usually possible to have hot *croissant* delivered in time for breakfast. All bakers open at least on Sunday morning, if not for the whole day, and for the first half of a public holiday. Cakes and tarts, especially, are expensive — although cheap by American standards — but the quality of the ingredients, variety and attractiveness of the presentation and the skill involved in their preparation warrant the price you pay.

Eating and Drinking, and Shopping

There are several different types of butchers in Belgium. There is the one who sells pork, beef and a little veal, all uncooked. From time to time he may prepare some sausages and perhaps a meat pâté. His shop is called a *boucherie/beenhouwerij*. Then there is the butcher who specialises in mutton and lamb but who probably sells some pork and a little beef as well. Again, the meat will be uncooked but he, too, may offer some preparations from time to time. His shop is called a *moutonnerie/slagers-schapevlees*. Then there is the butcher who sells mostly horse meat but with some pork and maybe another type of meat as well. His shop is known as a *boucherie chevaline/slager-paardevlees*. And, lastly, there is the *charcuterie/fijne vleeswaren* where you can buy all manner of cooked meats and preparations such as steak tartare (prepared or unprepared), a wide variety of sausages for cooking, pâtés, meat loaf and meat salad ready to take home for cooking or to eat cold. If you need a quick snack for lunch, *charcuteries* generally have a stock of crusty rolls (*pistolets*) and sometimes sliced bread (brown or white), which they will fill on request with cold meat or with one of their preparations to take away to eat.

These are the basic types of butchers; however, as people spend less and less time going from shop to shop, you will find that more and more butcher's shops are becoming less and less specialised and that many of those selling uncooked meat will offer a range of cold meats and many of the *charcuteries* will sell some uncooked meat.

Butchers cut meat very differently from British and American butchers. If you want those cuts there is one place to go and that is to Eddy's Meat Market in Watermael. However, once you understand the Belgian cuts it is very easy to find the right type of meat for the meal you plan to cook at a regular butcher's shop. If you are having meat cut especially it is best to be there when the butcher prepares your order so that you can make sure that it is right. For instance, if you ask for meat to be cut for a fondue the pieces may be too big for your requirements. The supermarket chain of Delhaize has a very good advertisement comparing the Belgian cuts of pork, beef and mutton with the British and American equivalents, which it publishes annually in *Living in Belgium & Luxembourg*.

Eating and Drinking, and Shopping

Pork is traditionally the meat the most often consumed in Belgium, particularly by the poorer people, and it is the cheapest meat available, apart from chicken. However, that does not mean that the quality is not good. There is some very good pork for sale but it is extremely difficult to buy belly of pork that will produce good crackling. If you want to stuff a joint of pork you can take your stuffing already prepared to the butcher and he will roll and tie it in for you. (You can do this at a butcher's shop; I have never tried it at a supermarket's butcher's counter, but I doubt that it would work.) Suckling pig, however, is considered a great delicacy.

The second most common meat is undoubtedly beef. Steaks figure high in the Belgian diet and they are very good, far better on the whole than those you will buy in the average British butcher's. There will be an absolute minimum of nerve and probably no fat at all. On the whole, the Belgians do not like fatty meat and a joint will usually be barded to make up for this deficiency.

A flavour similar to beef, although sweeter and much darker in colour but very popular, is horse meat. It is also considerably cheaper than beef. Horse meat is usually only available in specialised shops.

Veal is an extremely expensive meat and, consequently, more rarely eaten. It is generally sold as a roast or in wafer-thin slices and, more rarely, as cutlets.

Lamb and mutton are relative newcomers to the market. Unfortunately, the Belgians have been put off eating it for years by the inferior quality product with the yellow fat which lines the mouth for hours afterwards. Little differentiation is made between lamb and mutton; it is all generally classed as lamb. It is only recently that New Zealand and now British lamb and mutton have come onto the market and are becoming greatly appreciated. However, they are extremely expensive.

Game which once lived on the hoof is sold by just a few shops, although quite a few butcher's will sell domestic rabbits. It is really best to go to the Ardennes to purchase the various types of venison and the wild boar for which those forests are renowned. Both wild and domestic rabbits can be found, the latter being very common. Rabbit, especially hare, is considered a delicacy in

131

Eating and Drinking, and Shopping

Belgium. Game of the feathered variety, as well as poultry, is sold mostly by delicatessens or *traiteurs*. Pheasant, guinea fowl, quails, wild duck, goose and turkey are all common in season. The Belgians are much more precise than the British about the sex and age of a 'chicken': a baby bird is a *poussin/kuiken* and a *coquelet/haantje* is a very young *poussin*; a young chicken is a *poulet/jonge kip*; a capon, *chapon/kapoen* is a castrated cock; a *poularde/braadkip* is a carefully raised twenty-week old hen, of similar quality to a capon; a *poule/soepkip* and a *coq/haan* are about a year old and are not for roasting.

Many delicatessens sell fish in addition to game and poultry, as well as delicious dishes ready to serve or to pop into the oven. Delicatessens usually carry a stock of wines to serve with the types of food they specialise in and other tinned delicacies that can accompany the meal. The delicatessen's main function, however, is as an outside caterer. You can either collect your order or he will deliver it. For those who entertain and do not want to do the work themselves, the delicatessen is worth his weight in gold. He will prepare all manner of delights for a cocktail party or a full three-, four- or five-course meal just ready to pop into the oven, including all the drinks, depending on your budget. Not only will he supply the food but he will cook it in your home, supply the staff necessary for the preparation, serving and cleaning up afterwards, and even provide equipment that you may not have, such as tables and chairs, cloths, cutlery and just about anything you can think of that will contribute to making a first-class reception.

There are not many shops that sell only fish and, the farther you get from the sea, the less likely you are to find a fish shop. However, most parts of the country are covered by travelling fishmongers who tour a certain area on set days of the week. They drive down daily from the coast and you can be sure that what they have to sell is fresh. (In the same way, grocers and bakers have set rounds, too; the grocer replacing the British milkman, delivering milk, fruit and vegetables as well as groceries.)

Milk is not as good as in Britain in that there is very little cream content. Milk bought in a carton, except 'long life', should be turned out quickly into a jug as it does not

Eating and Drinking, and Shopping

keep very long in its packaging. Milk is bought from the general grocer's shop where you will also find eggs, cheese, dried and tinned foodstuffs, all types of beverages including wines and alcohols, and fruit and vegetables. The greengrocery of Britain is not known here.

Cheese shops are worth exploring when you find one for they are relatively few in major cities and rare elsewhere. They hold an enormous stock of cheeses from all over Europe, including Britain, but do try the numerous Belgian ones of which there is certainly something to appeal to every palate.

'Farm' shops have recently started to spring up selling salt-free bread, bread made from special cereals, non-industrially produced cheeses and cold meats, such as hams and sausages, and pâtés. The accent is on homemade rather than industrial production. There are a few health food shops which generally stock dietetic foods, too, although these are not so widely available as in Britain and their products are generally very expensive.

Ethnic food shops selling just about every type of foreign speciality certainly exist in Brussels but elsewhere only where a substantial population of the country has taken up residence. Even supermarkets in Brussels and the surrounding areas stock foods from Britain, France, Germany, the Netherlands, Italy, Spain and China on a regulr basis.

In addition to the small shops just mentioned, there are medium-sized self-service shops, supermarkets and hypermarkets. The self-service shops are small stores that have adapted to the system of letting the client browse at ease but are on hand to serve if required. In fact, for some items, such as fruit and vegetables, the shop assistant may serve you.

Since the advent of supermarkets, which now are to be found all over the country, life for the newly arrived expatriate is not likely to be too difficult because you can go into one of the Robs, Delhaizes, GBs or Nopris and have time to look around and compare different items without a shopkeeper hovering over you waiting to take your money. And, unless you have difficulty in finding what you are looking for, you will probably not have to say more than a thank you when you collect your change at the

Eating and Drinking, and Shopping

checkout. Even the habit of receiving change is beginning to die out with the installation of electronic devices at the checkout desk that read your bank account number from your plastic card and deduct the amount direct from your bank account.

In areas where there is a large concentration of foreigners many of the supermarkets stock goods from their native countries. The mark-up is not so high and it does enable you to eat traditionally from time to time. British goods are particularly easy to find in these stores.

Some supermarket-type stores exist where you can buy in bulk and obtain a discount, such as Colruyt. The only true discount house is Macro but to enter you need a special card, issued by the store, and this is only available to businesses, especially commerce.

There are one or two hypermarkets, such as the GB Maxis, where you can buy everything from a washing-machine to a piece of cheese. There are also some complexes consisting of supermarket, garden centre, brico centre and carpet warehouse.

Medicines in Belgium cannot be sold in anything but a chemist's and these sell little more than proprietary and specially prepared medicines that are prescribed by a doctor. The cheaper range of cosmetics and perfumes, household supplies such as paper handkerchiefs and cotton wool and cleaning materials, and items for personal hygiene are stocked by a *droguerie*, or 'drug store'. Expensive cosmetics and perfumes are to be found in a *parfumerie*.

One new English arrival recently confided that what she missed most of all was Boots. The nearest that one can find to Boots in Belgium is the chain of *drogueries* set up by the supermarket group of Delhaize Le Lion under the name of Super Di. There you can find a limited number of dietetic and health foods, household cleaning utensils and materials, toiletries and make-up but, of course, no medicines.

> Luxembourg city is perched on a spur which made it for centuries one of the strongest fortresses in Europe. An extraordinary network of underground tunnels and more than 40,000 sq m of casemates lie below the city. They were created to shelter the population, its possessions and horses in times of trouble (*Luxembourg National Tourist & Trade Office*)

Eating and Drinking, and Shopping

The old-fashioned ironmonger's shop is like Aladdin's cave and the place to go not just to find screws and the like but step-ladders, bottled gas, door and window frames and a host of other do-it-yourself type items. In the last few years, large-surface do-it-yourself stores, usually called 'brico centres', have sprung up. Depending on the size of the store, they will sell virtually anything you may need for home-improvement, your car and, perhaps, the construction of a building.

For clothes and shoes you will certainly be tempted by the attractive shop windows to look in small shops where you will find variety. Couturiers have a variety of models for you to try each season which can then be made up to your measurements in a fabric selected from their large stock. All-leather shoes are still to be found at reasonable prices. Hats are rarely worn by ladies and, consequently, you will see few milliners or millinery departments in large stores.

Fashions are perhaps different from those in Britain, even behind in time, but well followed. There has always been an influence from either the Germanic races or from Paris and the emphasis has always been on conservatism and quality. In the last few years, a definite Belgian style has crept into local fashion, particularly as worn by the younger generation. One of its most important features is the use and combination of colours not normally associated with classical styles.

There is not much choice in the department stores these days since most of them are under the same ownership. At one time Innovation, Grands Bazars and Au Bon Marché were all independent chains. Today, they are one: GB-Inno-BM and, of course, mostly stock the same merchandise.

Many people enjoy the thrill of markets, the search for something that pleases and the chance of picking it up

---

Luxembourg is a country of enormous natural beauty. It has much to offer the walker and those practising aquatic sports. The Sûre river cuts right through some of the most picturesque scenery and to follow its course can make an interesting itinerary. A pretty spot, popular with campers, climbers and walkers, is the small market town of Esch-sur-Sure (above), reached after passing through a tunnel in the rocks (*Luxembourg National Tourist & Trade Office*)

Eating and Drinking, and Shopping

cheaper than in a shop. You will find no end of outdoor markets in Belgium and many in Brussels itself, some held daily like the fruit and vegetable markets on the Place Ste Catherine, the Place Flagey or in the Parvis St Gilles. The biggest one is held on Sunday mornings around the Gare du Midi where there are large Greek and Arab communities and where you will find the ingredients and specialities of their cuisines, as well as clothing and household goods. There is a flower market every morning on the Grand'Place.

Other markets range from the antiques and book market held on the Grand Sablon on Saturdays and Sundays to the horse market held on the Place de la Duchesse every Friday until 2pm. On Sunday mornings, the Grand'Place is not only bright with colourful flowers but alive with bird song as the weekly bird mrket takes place. Then there are the flea markets, the most famous being held in Brussels' Place du Jeu de Balle each morning, but many others have sprung up on squares all over the city and in the towns round about. Some markets are held once a week, others once a fortnight or even once a month.

Specifically About Luxembourg

Gastronomy in Luxembourg is quite different from that of Belgium. There is a distinct Germanic influence in the nature of the local dishes and the cuisine cannot be compared with that of Belgium. However, that does not mean that you cannot eat well in the country. There are some very good eating houses in the capital and out in the country. Being so far from the sea, saltwater fish is rare. However, the icy-cold hillside streams are ideal for trout, and pike is caught in the Sûre, Moselle and Our rivers.

Pork is the most commonly eaten meat and is served in a variety of ways. Smoked, it is accompanied by a type of broad bean, and sausages and a type of black pudding comes with mashed potatoes and horseradish.

Sauerkraut is very popular, and one of the more unusual dishes has it served with calves' liver dumplings and boiled potatoes.

But Luxembourg's strongest gastronomic point is its wines. It has a good range of white Moselle wines that are

Eating and Drinking, and Shopping

not so sweet as the German variety from the other bank of that river. They have a pleasant bouquet and are ideal drinking for a warm summer's day. There is also a local beer industry.

The country is also noted for its fruit liqueurs, called in French an '*alcool blanc*' because of their clear, almost colourless nature. There are the traditional cherry (*kirsch*) and *poire Williams* type, but also a whole variety of plum drinks.

When you are shopping for food in Luxembourg there is not the variety of types of butchers that there is in Belgium. Fish shops are understandably scarce.

In Luxembourg city, there is just one rather small supermarket, near the station, but outside in the country there are much bigger ones selling an enormous variety of goods.

It should be pointed out that shopping in Luxembourg for all manner of items is especially interesting because of the low rate of VAT put on them, but particularly for alcohols, cigarettes, furs, cars, leather goods, perfume and other luxury goods. (Petrol is also very much cheaper.) In order to attract custom from over its borders, the authorities purposely practise a policy of maintaining prices slightly under those of its neighbours.

11
Travelling Around

You will find it extremely easy to journey around within Belgium whether or not you have your own transport. There is a very good and relatively efficient network of public transport services and rail and road communications are highly developed. However, it is more convenient to have your own vehicle and you will find that cars are generally cheaper here than in Britain because Belgium is not subject to the same constraints on distribution.

You may go to any dealer to buy a car and, depending on the make and model, you will usually receive it within a few weeks. It is relatively easy to purchase a right-hand drive vehicle should you wish to, although some dealers try to restrict deliveries of these models as they realise that the final destination of many is the British Isles and that the purchaser has succeeded in paying a lower price than he would normally do by going through the usual channels. In fact, if you plan to live on the continent for a year or more, you would be ill-advised to buy a right-hand drive car as it is far more easy to drive a left-hand drive vehicle in countries which drive on the right.

Normally, when you buy a car from a dealer you will be required to sign a contract and pay a small deposit when you give your order. The cost of the vehicle is subject to Belgian VAT at the rate of 25 per cent but this will have been included in the price quoted to you at the outset. You will be required to pay the outstanding amount on receipt of your car.

Unless you are buying direct from the showroom, and that is possible from some distributors, you will probably have to wait a few weeks to take delivery of your car. Once it is in production, you will be notified by the distributor that you can collect the papers that will set the whole process of putting the vehicle on the road in motion. The papers consist of a request for registration and will indicate the type of car, its horsepower and the chassis number. It is then up to you to fill in the details of ownership and to affix the correct amount of fiscal stamps (bought at the post office), each of which must be defaced with your signature. The document should then be sent or taken, for quickness, to your insurance company or agent.

Third party insurance is compulsory and the very minimum that you are required to cover by law. You will be issued with a 'green card' which is, in effect, a piece of green paper and states the period and in which countries the vehicle is covered. The driver is legally bound to carry this with him and must never leave it in the vehicle.

You would be most unwise to drive in Belgium with just third party insurance unless your vehicle is old. Certainly for a new car, or one that is just two or three years old, it is best to take out a fully comprehensive insurance with all the extras, such as legal aid, fire and theft which are not automatically covered by such a policy. Car insurance is very expensive but, if you agree to sign up with an insurance company for ten years, you can obtain a slight reduction on the premium.

Most policies require the holder to pay the first so many thousand francs' damage in the case where an accident claim has been filed against him. This provision, called a deductible by Americans, is determined at the moment the policy is drawn up. Of course, the bigger the provision, the smaller the premium.

Your insurance company or broker will issue you with standard accident forms for use in the event of a collision. This document does not incriminate either party but simply makes sure that all the necessary information is gathered together and in a standard way which saves time. It is wise to keep a spare form with the car documents. The form does exist in English, and it would be wise to request one for reference.

Having filled in the front side of the form to each other's satisfaction, one person keeps the original and the other takes the copy. The reverse side of your copy you can fill in at home afterwards and then mail it or take it to your

Travelling Around

insurance company along with an explanatory letter. Only if someone is injured or if there is any dispute should you call the police or the gendarmerie. In many cases it is better to call the latter as they have jurisdiction throughout the country, whereas the police works only locally.

Do not have your vehicle repaired until the insurance company tells you that you may do so. However, the company will require an estimate of the cost of the repairs involved and you should ask for this in writing from your garage. if there is a fair amount of damage done an assessor will need to see the car. As soon as he has seen the car you can arrange for its repair. When the work is completed, it will be up to you to pay the bill and then take or send the original invoice to the insurance company for reimbursement. Of course, should you be unlucky enough to have a 'write-off' then the insurance company will pay up once the value of the vehicle has been agreed. However, whatever the sum involved, do not expect to receive your money quickly, particularly if you pass the file through your broker. The whole operation does take time.

But to return to the procedure for buying your vehicle. Having arranged for coverage, the insurance company will complete a form which must then be submitted to the transport department of the Ministry of Communications together with the customs clearance document provided by the seller. This will permit you to obtain an official number plate. It will also put into motion the process for paying the road tax. You receive no document to display or keep in your vehicle as proof of payment of that tax, but you will be given a 'virement' form which will state how much your car has been rated at, the amount to pay and by which date. Failure to pay on time will result in a fine.

Normally, the number plate will be sent to you through the post, together with a long grey document, commonly known as the *carte grise/grijse kaart* because of its greyish colour, which is the registration card or log-book. You are now free to collect your vehicle. Only one plate will have been issued, bearing a specially embossed mark, and this must be fitted to the rear of the car. The second, which has to be fitted to the front of your vehicle, can be made up by a garage or accessory shop.

Belgian law requires you to carry at all times in your

Travelling Around

vehicle the following items: a workable fire extinguisher, a red triangle to indicate a breakdown, and a first-aid kit containing certain specific items (which can be purchased from a chemist). Cars must be fitted with a red high-density fog lamp at the rear and seat belts for the two front seats. The wearing of safety belts in the front seats is compulsory at all times, and children under twelve must never travel in the front part of the car, but must sit behind. Since the beginning of 1986 all new cars have to have wing mirrors fitted to both sides of the vehicle.

If you are only going to be residing a short time in Belgium and do not particularly want to buy a left-hand drive car you could lease one for the duration of your stay. There are a number of companies that provide such a service which, depending on the length of time you are planning to lease the vehicle, can cost about the same as buying. Nor is it necessary to have a large limousine as the companies lease all types and sizes of cars.

However, perhaps you are intending to import a car that you have already owned and used for more than six months. If so, before you can change the number plates there are several steps that must be taken. If the car has been declared by the removal company on the inventory of goods being imported, the necessary forms to be filled in for the car will be supplied automatically and a good remover will do the work for you.

The regulations pertaining to the importing of vehicles tend to change more frequently than probably any other piece of information contained in this book. Consequently, anyone organising his own importation of a vehicle should check first with the Belgian customs office that the following information is still valid. At the moment you will start the procedure by obtaining forms 133, 139B and three copies of 48-TER from the Belgian customs office. These forms need to be completed and presented, together with photocopies of all the car's present documents — registration and insurance papers, and, if possible, invoice — and a letter, preferably in French or Dutch, requesting permission to import the vehicle, to the head of customs. You will also be required to supply form 136, which is the document relating to the importation of your goods.

Travelling Around

You will receive in return, one copy of form 133 and half of the document 139B. These cover you for three months and can be – and should be if you do not hear from customs in time – extended.

The next step is to have the vehicle converted to Belgian specifications. For this you should go to the manufacturer's national importer and ask for the necessary changes to be made, and for a Certificate of Conformity. Having accomplished this, the vehicle will have to go through the local technical inspection, known as the Technical Control where you will be required to hand over the form 133. All Belgian cars over four years old have to pass this test annually, too, as well as newly purchased second-hand vehicles. The Technical Control testing centres are all state run and do nothing else but test the road-worthiness of vehicles and act as examination centres for new drivers. They are very well organised and the equipment used is extremely accurate.

Having passed the test and completed all the requirements, you are now in a position to go, in person, to the Ministry of Communications to obtain your Belgian licence plates and to receive a temporary permission to import the vehicle. Eventually, you will receive a letter from customs and you should send them back all the documents they require. It can take from nine months to two years from the outset that you will receive a letter from them granting permission to import your car without paying TVA or taxes. At this point, you return to the customs office with the forms 133 and 19B which are exchanged for a 136 and a card 705, which allows you to change the temporary registration to a permanent one. The licence plates, however, remain the same.

You will have gathered that there is a lot of red tape involved, particularly in importing a used car, and there are companies that are specialised in this work and will take care of it for you – for a fee, of course.

Rules of the Road

Driving in Belgium is quite different from at home and requires extreme caution. National driving licences have been in existence less than twenty years and, when they did come into being, they were acquired by paying BF250

Travelling Around

and signing an affidavit that you had driven before. Consequently, there are still a large number of drivers on the roads who have never passed a test, and some who probably would not pass it if they had to take it now. Belgians are generally much better motorway drivers than the British since they are taught to drive on these roads. However, Britons and Americans usually have some problems in adapting to the style of city driving which is quite aggressive.

As long as you drive to the Belgian highway code you are protected. Therefore, it is extremely important to obtain a copy quickly, as soon as you arrive. Unfortunately, it is no longer available in English but can be obtained in French or Dutch from major book shops. The motoring clubs can also provide information.

Basically, the things you must be aware of are the international road signs which are used and the speed limits. Both should be respected and are quite frequently controlled. There are heavy fines for not adhering to the laws, especially those infractions which are considered criminal offences. There are fourteen of these which are, loosely translated:

1 Failure to obey the orders of someone authorised to enforce the law; that is, a policeman, military police, gendarme, *garde-champêtre*, etc.
2 Failure to respect the laws relating to priority; not giving way, not stopping and not giving way at a stop sign.
3 Failure to respect the laws relating to passing vehicles; not respecting sign B19 — two arrows, one white (indicating priority) and the other red on a blue background (obligation to give way to drivers coming from the opposite (white) direction).
4 Overtaking on the left a driver who had indicated his intention to turn left and who had moved out to the left in order to execute the turn; overtaking whilst the driver could not see sufficiently far ahead other vehicles coming in the opposite direction; overtaking on the approach to a summit or in a bend when overtaking is indicated as being forbidden; overtaking, when overtaking was forbidden, a driver who was himself overtaking another vehicle, other than a bicycle, moped or two-wheeled

145

Travelling Around

motorcycle; not respecting the sign forbidding the overtaking of a vehicle of more than two wheels and that forbidding drivers of transport vehicles whose maximum authorised weight exceeds 3½ tons, to overtake a vehicle with more than two wheels.
5 Overtaking or drawing level with on the left a vehicle on rails (tram or tramways' maintenance car) when overtaking or drawing level with a vehicle was forbidden.
6 When changing direction:
   putting other drivers in danger during the normal movement of the traffic;
   impeding drivers coming from the opposite direction;
   not giving way to the normal traffic and other road users.
7 Placing a pedestrian in danger.
8 Driving more than 10kph (6mph) over the maximum authorised speed.
9 Driving a motorised vehicle, bicycle, etc without lights before or behind whilst the use of lights is obligatory.
10 Using a gap on a motorway to make a U-turn; or reversing on a motorway.
11 Entering a level crossing area when it is forbidden, that is, when the red light shows.
12 Not respecting (stopping at) a red or permanently orange light.
13 Crossing a continuous white line separating the lines of traffic.
14 Not respecting the sign C24 forbidding access into cities to drivers of vehicles carrying dangerous merchandise.

The punishment for committing one or several of these infractions depends on the gravity and the number of points infringed. However, the law provides for fairly hefty fines and or imprisonment from eight days to a month. In addition, the driving licence can be immediately retracted by the King's Prosecutor and the judge can pronounce the forfeiture of the right to drive.

If you have changed your driving licence for a Belgian one, as you must do within three months of being resident in the country, you cannot use ignorance as the excuse if you fail to obey a signal or if you cause an accident. In order to obtain your driving licence, you sign a statement saying that you are cognizant with the Belgian highway code.

Apart from giving way to vehicles coming from the right where they have priority, the most urgent rule you will need to learn quickly is not to argue with a tram or a bus. Trams have absolute priority and buses, while one is supposed to give way to them when they indicate they are moving away from a stop, the city ones use their size to force their way through. And, should you have an accident with either service, you will have great difficulty in extracting reimbursement. You should also give way to ambulances, fire appliances and police cars that are sounding their sirens or have their blue lights flashing.

In comparison, the other differences in driving between Belgium and Britain are relatively small. For example, it is the law that you must not drive on side lights only. Side lights are only recognised as a 'parking' light and, if you are involved in an accident at night and only have your side lights switched on, this will go against you. In an accident in bad weather, the fact that you have your side lights switched on will not count in your favour. When moving, you should either have your full, but dimmed, headlights turned on, or nothing at all depending on the conditions.

You will be well advised never to flash your headlights and always to be wary of anyone who flashes his headlights at you as, in Belgium, this usually means 'you are in my way' or 'I am taking the priority', and not, as in Britain, 'I am giving way to you'.

Park your car at all times of the day on the side of the road, facing the way the traffic on that side is travelling. It is illegal to park it facing the other direction. If you park on a meter you will be well advised to feed it: parking fines are quite expensive and necessitate buying special 'fine' stamps at the post office, sticking them onto the document you find on your windscreen, defacing them with your signature, and returning one half to the issuing police station.

Some cities and communes use a disc system for parking, although this is dying out as more and more authorities are after making money by selling parking

Travelling Around

space. The discs can be purchased for a few francs from local garages, shops, banks and tourist offices. You set the disc to the time of your arrival and it automatically shows the time you should leave (within two hours).

In other places, there are machines, similar to those to be found in Britain, from which you can buy tickets authorising you to stay for the length of time you indicate. The ticket here comes in two parts, one of which you leave on your dashboard so that the authorities can see it, the other you take with you as a reminder as it shows the time by which you should depart.

When parking in streets without meters, discs, or machines, beware. There are different signs, explained in the highway code, as to where you can park and when. It may be that you can only park on one side of a road on certain days.

Yellow lines are not for parking on, nor are pavements (even one or two wheels) unless indicated, corners of streets (up to 5m (5½yd) either side) and entrances to private property.

The speed limit in built-up areas is 60kph (37mph), except where otherwise indicated. The restriction starts where the white name-board is placed at the entrance to the village, town or city, and ends where the white name-board bearing a red slash through it is placed on leaving the area. Out of town, the speed limit is 90kph (56mph) on regular roads and 120kph (74mph) on motorways and fast roads with at least two lanes in each direction. This may be changed in the future to 110kph (68mph) on fast roads and 130kph (80mph) on motorways. Failure to observe the speed limit can be an expensive business, too.

Belgium's motorways are mostly very well equipped with service stations, lighting and emergency telephones. Many of the big rest areas have a service station, cafeteria and toilets. Emergency telephones are situated at regular intervals on both sides, and arrows affixed to the central lamp post indicate in which direction the nearest telephone can be found.

The several motoring organisations offer good services to their clients and are worth joining. The largest one, the Touring Club (the equivalent of the British AA), offers the best coverage over the whole country, while the RCAB,

Travelling Around

Royal Automobile Club de Belgique (the equivalent of the British RAC), is second in importance and also covers the whole country but is stronger in Wallonia.

For those who travel abroad regularly, membership of Mondial Assistance or Europ Assistance offer such advantages as financial help in an emergency, medical aid and repatriation of an injured person and the vehicle if necessary.

Public Transport
City transport is very good. Both Brussels and Antwerp have underground systems, known here as the 'metro'.

The Brussels metro was begun in the late sixties and there is now a well-developed network of lines. Special, very smart orange and silver trains run on the completed sections, while trams vanish down holes in the ground on routes that have yet to be finished. All the stations are covered, even where the lines run over ground, and every one is different. Many stations are decorated with works of art by Belgium's major contemporary artists.

Above ground, city services are maintained by a bus and tram network with some of the trams entering the 'pre-metro' circuit. Many of the trams are articulated and some of the modern buses, too.

There is one price and one type of ticket that is valid for metro, bus or tram in Brussels. You can change transport, too, as long as you are making an on-going journey and not returning, all for the same price and within one hour of setting out. It is easiest and cheapest, unless you are using public transport several times a day, to buy a 'card' of ten journeys which gives you a saving of about a third of the single journey fare. Cards can be purchased at the ticket office at metro stations and in some newspaper kiosks.

Metro trains stop at every station but buses and trams are obliged to stop only at 'halts'. In between, there are 'request' stops when the driver should be flagged down. You should be careful by which door you get on public transport. You can enter a metro train by any door because your ticket will have been clipped before you make your way onto the platform. When climbing on a bus or tram or 'pre-metro' tram, you should enter at the front

149

Travelling Around

of the vehicle and punch your ticket immediately or give the driver the fare — as near as possible to the exact amount. The public transport system is patrolled by inspectors who have the right to fine you and demand payment on the spot if your ticket is not in order. When you want to alight from a metro train it will stop at the station in question but you may have to push the button to open the door nearest to you. In trams and buses, look up to ceiling level where you will see a 'halt' sign which lights up if someone else has made the request before you. Should your door not open when the vehicle has stopped moving, ring again to draw the driver's attention to the fact.

Metro maps are clearly displayed on the underground system rather as in London; it is not always easy to find out what buses and trams go where as maps are generally only displayed at major stops. If you intend using the public transport service regularly, you would be well advised to obtain a map of the city's transport services which, for Brussels, can be obtained from the STIB/MIVB kiosk at the Porte de Namur metro station.

A much more expensive way of moving around is by taxi. However, there is one advantage and that is that the tip is included in the cost, and so you should not add anything on top. Most taxis are radio-cabs, others operate from special ranks located at strategic points around the cities. Consequently, you should telephone for a vehicle or go to a stand-point.

A separate bus service operates to places outside the city limits and this is run by a different company. It relates most closely to the British country bus system although these are generally operated by the same company as the city buses.

For longer distances there is a well-integrated train and bus network, the buses operating where the trains cannot penetrate. There are three types of regular, national network train: local (L), meaning 'slow' and which stops virtually everywhere; inter-regional (IR) and inter-city (IC) trains do not stop at all stations but inter-regional ones stop more frequently than the inter-city ones. Then there are peak-hour trains (P), which are added to the normal schedule to help commuters and are invariably faster even

Travelling Around

than inter-city ones, and, in the summer months, tourist trains (T), which are slotted in as timetables allow.

In addition to the national trains, some of which go over the border into neighbouring countries, there are international trains on all the main lines, some of which originate in Belgium, others coming to Belgium from other countries, and a large number passing through. There is nothing to stop you getting on one of these if it serves the stations you require. It will be faster than most of the local network and, should there be any delays, it will be given priority in order not to upset other countries' schedules. However, generally, trains do run to time and they can never leave the station earlier than their schedule permits.

Intercity and international services have two classes, except for the trans-European expresses (TEE), which have one class but for which there is a supplement added to the first-class price. Seats on the TEE trains must be booked in advance and standing is not allowed.

If you travel regularly by railway between two destinations it may be in your interest to buy a season ticket. These are available for different lengths of time and usually require a passport photograph. There are special season tickets, too, which allow you to travel by rail any five days during a two-week period and anywhere you want within the country. Special rates exist for students on all forms of Belgian transport and for large families. Details on how to obtain special tickets can be obtained from your local station.

Specifically About Luxembourg

Owning a car in Luxembourg is very similar to owning a car in Belgium in that the same administrative procedures need to be adhered to. For vehicle registration you will need to apply initially to the Plateau du St Esprit in the capital, and registration is eventually obtained from the offices at 1-3 avenue Guillaume. Vehicle inspection takes place at the Ministry of Transport's premises at Sandweiler, on the way to the country's eastern border, and the road tax should be paid to the Bureau des Contributions.

Fines issued by the police for driving offences can be

Travelling Around

paid by cheque or by 'virement'.

It is more usual to telephone for a taxi in the capital since there are only one or two stand-points. Vehicles come very quickly and it is often easier to use a taxi than drive a car since parking is at a premium.

Public transport in the capital is served by a very good bus service which operates out of the bus station on the corner of the Rue Aldringer. The rest of the country is served by a network of trains and buses.

12
Getting to Know the Country

Belgium is a country full of riches; one that is able to provide a wide range of interests for visitors despite its small area. In winter, you can ski in the hills of the Ardennes — referred to locally as mountains although they do not quite make it in height — when there is snow on the several slopes, that is. Cross-country skiing, however, is much more certain and becoming well developed, and there are some lovely trails to explore through the wooded areas of the south. And, when the sun shines — even in spring if you are lucky — you can get a very good suntan from lying in the sand dunes up at the coast.

All the year round there are the museums, art galleries and exhibitions to visit. Many of the finest old master works were painted in Belgium — the Brueghels and Rubens, for example — and a good number can still be admired in the country's museums. Belgians are naturally artistic: the skill is not something which confined itself to one or two generations of their ancestors but it has been passed on down through the centuries. Nor is this artistic side limited only to painting and sculpture: furniture, ceramics and architecture are just a few of the forms in which it is expressed. Even shop windows are dressed with incredibly good taste.

When you look down a list of permanent collections you will think that there is a museum for everything — and you will not be far wrong. In addition to the more common collections of art, lace, military souvenirs, cars and the like, there are museums housing playing cards, bicycles, flax, iron and coal, beer and diamonds, to name just a few.

But nothing can beat the countryside for variety and interest. If you start at the cost, which is little more than 70km (43 miles) long, you will find that each resort and village is different. Ostend, the major port for the cross-

Getting to Know the Country

Channel ferries and home of the small Belgian navy, is unpretentiously commercial and lacks the chic of the other highly popular resort to its north, Knokke-Le Zoute. But Ostend, home town of the famous Belgian painter of a British father, James Ensor, nevertheless boasts a casino, too. Another of its great attractions is its fishing port with a quayside fish market.

No need to prepare a picnic before setting out; you can purchase those big Dublin Bay prawns (known locally as *langoustines*), or freshly caught shrimps and unshelled prawns at the market, buy a stick of French bread and a bottle of wine or some beer in a nearby grocer's shop, and take them onto the beach, or drive south down the coast to a quieter resort, such as Koksijde, and find a sheltered corner in the dunes. In fact, you can even take your prawns onto one of the café terraces opposite Ostend fish market, order something to drink, and the waiter will probably bring a plate to take the empty shells.

At Oostduinkerke, towards the French border, shrimp fishermen still ride out on horseback into the sea with large baskets strapped either side of the saddle to make their catch. On the third Sunday in June there is an annual Shrimp Festival which includes a shrimp-fishing contest between the fishermen, a fishermen's market and a shrimp parade.

Up the coast towards Holland you will find the Zwin, a large marshy nature reserve with a large collection of bird-life that will interest ornithologists. It is the summer nesting ground of a small number of storks and on the migration routes of many coastal birds.

The flat lands of Flanders, so well depicted by the Flemish old masters, start at the coast and stretch inland almost to Brussels in one direction and to the French border in another. They have hardly changed over the years: sleepy rivers and canals lined by willow trees abound, and prosperous market towns with their typical step-gabled buildings dot the rural areas at strategic crossing points on the old trade routes.

It is in this type of countryside that Bruges (or to give it its proper name, Brugge) lies. Variously called the 'Jewel of Belgium' and the 'Venice of the North', both of which are apt titles, Bruges was an important Hanseatic port

Getting to Know the Country

until it became silted up. Its city fathers are fortunately extremely conscious of the value of their inheritance and do everything to preserve its beauty while being realistic enough to accept the fact that tourisim is of considerable importance to its new-found wealth.

When you visit Bruges, please do not merely take a boat ride on the canals and wander aimlessly around its cobbled streets. Do visit the beautiful Basilica of the Holy Blood, where the faithful can venerate some drops of the blood of Christ at given times, and its small museum, as well as the Stadhuis (town hall), the Groeninge and Gruuthuse museums, and the Sint Jan Hospitaal. The latter contains the most incredible collection of works by Memling. You should also see the peaceful Begijnhof, close to the Minnewater, which housed a lay sisterhood. The *béguinages/begijnhoven* are special to Belgium and were walled-in communities of women who devoted themselves mainly to charitable works.

Bruges has several festivals, not all of them held every year. However, if you want to see some of the best pageantry in the country, you should not miss the 'Procession of the Holy Blood', which takes place each Ascension Day, and include a number of moving *tableaux*, depicting Bible scenes leading up to the death of Christ, which precede the reliquary of the Holy Blood through the streets. The other magnificent procession staged by the city takes place every five years and depicts its own history. Known as the Procession of the Golden Tree, it recalls the magnificent wedding of Charles the Bold, Duke of Normandy and Count of Flanders, to Princess Margaret of York, which was celebrated in the old Hanseatic city of Bruges in 1468. The next occasion on which the Procession of the Golden Tree will be performed is in the summer of 1990.

South from Bruges, heading for the French border, you will come to Courtrai, as it is known to us and the French, and as Kortrijk to the Flemish inhabitants. It is a pleasant, bustling town situated on the River Leie, and owes much of its wealth to the Middle Ages when it was an important centre for the retting of flax. Because of this business, which grew up along the banks, the river became known as the 'Golden Leie'.

Getting to Know the Country

Courtrai lies in the west of Flanders on the edge of what was one of the main theatres in World War I: the numerous cemeteries bear witness. In the thick is Ypres, as we and the French refer to the Flemish town of Ieper. It was many times besieged during its history before being destined to serve as a battleground three times in World War I. Today, it is a peaceful town that has much dignity and it is hard to imagine that, when the armies of the Great War had finished with it, they left behind them just the cobbled streets and a pile of rubble. The valiant locals, as their ancestors had done time and time before them, picked themselves up and rebuilt the town, faithfully copying the one that had been ravaged. For their courage, the town was awarded the British Military Cross, and the people continue to remember their dead, and those of the other armies, each night at the Menin Gate when the Last Post is sounded.

There is a strange custom in Ypres that takes place each year on the second Sunday in May, called the Festival of the Cats. The animals, nowadays cloth ones, are thrown to the crowd from the belfry in the continuation of a tradition started when live cats were thrown out, having served their purpose of keeping down the mice in the cloth hall where the wool was stored in winter.

Another market town in this region is Veurne (Furnes to the French). It has a vast, highly commercial square at ground level but from the first floor upwards the buildings have changed little since the seventeenth century. On the last Sunday in July a moving 'Procession of the Penitents' is held here. The local people put on sackcloth and ashes and re-enact Christ's journey to Calvary, each participant carrying a heavy wooden cross and many going barefoot.

Moving east across the northern part of the country you come to Ghent which conceals its beauty a little more protectively than the blatantly exhibitionist Bruges. For Ghent (spelt 'Gent' by its inhabitants) does not have to rely so heavily on tourism for its living. Lying at the confluence of the Scheldt and Leie rivers, it has built up over the centuries a tradition as a trading port, and is now an important inland harbour serving a number of new industries, including the oil refineries, that have grown up in the zone close by. The majority of tourists make the

Getting to Know the Country

journey to Ghent to admire Van Eyck's 'Adoration of the Mystic Lamb', which is housed in St Baaf's Cathedral and considered to be the chief work of the early Flemish School. However, having made the pilgrimage you should not neglect the wonderful old edifices of such buildings as the Cloth Hall (Lakenhalle), the Castle of the Counts of Flanders ('s Gravensteen) and the houses on the Graslei, many of which date back to the twelfth, thirteenth and fourteenth centuries.

Ghent, known as the 'City of Flowers', is famous for its azaleas, displayed every five years in a magnificent Chelsea-type show and grown in the surrounding region. (The next 'Floralies', as the show is called, will be held in 1990.) Another flower which has brought considerable wealth and colour to the area is the begonia, and that industry is centred on the nearby town of Lochristi. An annual begonia festival is held in Lochristi in August.

Flanders has a long tradition of painting and it is one that is still very much alive. If you follow the Leie river from Ghent a few miles in the direction of its source, you will come across the village of St-Martens-Latem, with a fifteenth-century windmill; a quiet corner, except on Sundays when it is invaded by the people of Ghent. Since the late nineteenth century it has been the home of some of Belgium's most famous artists and of whom Constant Permeke is probably the best known. It is unique in that you can visit the art galleries and then step outside into the countryside depicted in some of the works.

North-east of Ghent, and closer to the Scheldt estuary, lies Antwerp, one of Europe's leading ports and an extremely important centre for the cutting and polishing of diamonds. It is another beautiful city, with a very old heart, and, like Ghent, is not so well known to tourists. The main area of interest lies within a semi-circle formed nowadays by wide, tree-lined boulevards but which follow the line of ancient city ramparts. The city is the home of Rubens and you can visit his delightful patrician house and studio just off the Meir, the main shopping street, but you will find more of his works in the cathedral, too. Walking in the streets of the old part around the cathedral, and up to the strangely shaped but elegant main square or Grote Markt, has been made far more

Getting to Know the Country

pleasant since it has become reserved for pedestrians only.

It is easy to walk miles in Antwerp because all the points of interest look so close when you see them on a map: the fascinating Plantin-Moretus Museum, one of Europe's oldest printing houses, in the Vrijdag Markt; the Mayer van den Bergh Museum, with its impressive collection of paintings, on the Lange Gasthuisstraat; the Torengebouw, Europe's first skyscraper, on the Meir; and the Baroque St-Carolus-Borromeuskerk, whose magnificent west front is said to have been designed by Rubens, on the St Katelijneveest. But, when you are ready for a rest, make your way to the Scheldt and sit beside the Steen, now the National Maritime Museum, and watch the ships go by or, better still, take a sightseeing boat, some of which go as far as the string of islands belonging to Holland in the estuary.

If you walk down the Meir and across the boulevards that encircle the old town, it will lead you to the De Keyserlei and the diamond area, synonymous with the black hats, black suits, long beards and side curls of the Jewish population. The De Keyserlei ends at the immense Central Station, right beside which, surprisingly, you will find the zoo. While this section is the main part and typical of such establishments constructed last century, the much less formal part, set in an enormous country park, lies a short drive away, at Planckendael, close to Mechelen. It is there that the animals are sent to rest and recuperate, as well as to breed. Spring-time at Planckendael, with all the young animals and birds, presents a charming scene.

Another area of interest to nature-lovers in the Antwerp area lies to the north of the city and close to the Dutch border. The Kalmthoutse Heide, just 2km (1¼ miles) from the village of Kalmthout, consists of a vast sandy heathland which has been made into a nature reserve, primarily for the conservation of rare plants but which is also frequented by large numbers of birds.

There are two other nature reserves in the north of the country where you can spend the day peacefully walking but these are farther to the west. One is the rugged Mechelse Heide close to the German border, and the other

Getting to Know the Country

is the more commercial Molenheide, with its game park, not far from the racing track of Zolder. Also in this region, which is in the province of Limburg, is the domain of Bokrijk. While only partly a nature reserve, Bokrijk's biggest attraction is its museum of the open air consisting of over one hundred old rural buildings, nearly all of them from the province and the others from the rest of the northern part of the country, and including a charming, small twelfth-century church and several different types of windmill.

The regions mentioned so far, together with the northern part of Brabant province, make up the Flemish part of the country and form a natural language frontier across Belgium. Brussels is roughly in the middle of the country, a bilingual island in the Flemish part of the province of Brabant, which is French-speaking at its southernmost end. As you travel down from the coast or from Antwerp a gentle change takes place: there are distinctive hills, fewer expanses of water, market gardening, a great concentration of motorways and other roads converging on, and a few circling, the capital and elegant residential areas.

Despite first impressions from the road, which are likely to be of a glass and concrete metropolis, you will find that not all the old part of Brussels has been destroyed to make way for the new. There is a great movement of washing of old edifices, both private and public, and the result is spectacular. And, despite the concrete and glass towers, the beauty of the old buildings refuses to be diminished. You should seek out, in addition to the natural tourist areas of the Grand'Place, the Ilôt Sacré (Sacred Islet) and the Sablon areas, the Solvay House in the Avenue Louise (only for viewing from the outside), the Horta Museum which was the architect's home and studio, the Erasmus House, the Abbaye de la Cambre (now a famous art school) and the museums at the Cinquantenaire. And there are one or two of the modern constructions that one cannot but admire: the spectacular Modern Art Museum, for example, with its incredible use of space and light; and the Glaverbel and Royale Belge buildings, both in Boitsfort.

There are one hundred parks in Brussels and the city

Getting to Know the Country

has produced a useful map showing the amenities available at each. Many of the communes take the trouble to plant boxes or beds of flowers in the summer to add extra colour, and the flower carpet, spread over the whole of the Grand'Place in mid August is not to be missed. Another, annual floral event is the opening to the public of the royal greenhouses at Laken during certain hours in the month of May.

Brussels, or rather the elite association of the Ommegang, which is made up of Belgium's noblesse, stages an annual pageant in the magnificent setting of the Grand'Place on the first Thursday evening in July. It is a colourful re-enactment of the ceremony held in 1549 before Charles Quint and his sister Eleanor, widow of François I, and includes fashionable entertainment of the time such as flag throwing and stilt walking.

Another annual event takes place early in August and that is the planting of the 'May tree'. This is a particularly local event which involves the inhabitants of one very old area behind the national bank. August is also the month of the 'Foire du Midi', a popular fun fair held along the Boulevard du Midi with local specialities such as *beignets* vying with candy-floss and ice-creams, rifle ranges and other side shows, as well as big dippers and giant wheels.

A traditional military parade takes place in front of the in-town palace on the national day, 21 July. It is usually presided over by the king.

There are many places on the outskirts of Brussels that you will want to see and Waterloo has to be high on your list of priorities. Most British people will inevitably be disappointed for generally the tours and the sites where guides are available leave you in considerable doubt as to whether or not Wellington did actually win the great battle. You will need to visit the museum that bears the duke's name in the centre of the town to be reassured.

One of the things that the province of Brabant is noted for is its castle-farms: enormous strongholds of imposing houses and farm buildings enclosed behind a high red-brick wall containing one enormous entrance, now often completed by a set of elegant wrought-iron gates. You will certainly see some around Waterloo and also if you take the direction for Ronquières, the incredible engineering

Getting to Know the Country

feat that moves barges up the side of a hill, or for the picturesque ruins of the important Cistercian abbey of Villers-la-Ville.

Lying immediately south of Brussels is the Forêt de Soignes, all that remains at this point of the once continuous belt of forest that stretched from eastern Europe, through Germany, to the Ardennes and then on to Brussels. It is a favourite place for walking and riding with the people of Brussels at weekends.

The Sambre and Meuse rivers effectively cut off the south of the country from the rest. Everything below this line, with the exception of the province of Hainaut in the west, forms the Belgian Ardennes (in Belgium the name is used in the plural, whereas across the border in France they call their side l'Ardenne). It is a magnificently hilly region, forested in the south and east, and cut into by several old meandering rivers. The population, in comparison with the flat north, is sparsely spread and there are few major towns.

The two rivers formed a natural line to defend and the cliff faces of the higher banks provided ideal vantage points from which to cover invaders for many a century. Hence, the towns of Dinant, Namur and Huy, constructed at convenient bridging points along the valley, all have citadels from which the towns below were defended. The châteaux of the region, too, were hard to attack: Aigremont, was built on a pinnacle overlooking the Meuse, and Jehay-Bodegnée and Franc-Waret, a few kilometres from the Meuse, were both well moated.

Further east along the Meuse you arrive at Liège, once a principality owning lands stretching from inside present-day Holland and down to France, and ruled over by a prince-bishop. A beautiful city, containing some magnificent old treasures in its lofty churches and well-arranged museums, it is situated in a mining region and has an important inland port serving its various industries. If you visit Liège on a Sunday, make sure that you get there before lunch, in time to see the enormous open-air market which seems to sell everything that you can conceive in the area it encloses on the Quai de Maastricht and along the whole of the Quai de la Batte, after which it is named.

From Liège you can climb up to the heights of the

eastern part of the country, known as the Hautes Fagnes, much of which is Germanic by origin and of tongue. It is of particular interest to naturalists, being a high, marshy land with some unique fauna and flora. You can walk for miles here but it is dangerous to stray from the paths as you can easily find yourself in a bog.

Lenten carnivals are great festivals in the Ardennes and the most important in the Germanic part of the country takes place in Eupen on the Monday preceding Ash Wednesday, 'Rosenmontag'.

One of the best ways to see all the places and scenery of interest when driving in Belgium is to follow the special tourist routes that have been mapped out in certain places. You will recognise them by the hexagonal signs along the roadside, and there is generally a brochure or book about the route explaining what to look out for and the history of any buildings mentioned. You can either buy this documentation in a local bookshop or obtain it from the nearest tourist office. Probably the prettiest, and possibly the longest, of these routes is that of 'Ourthe and Aisne', following for a large part the two rivers bearing those names which lie to the south of Liège. The way takes you through gentle wooded countryside, tiny villages and to fascinating places such as Durbuy, the smallest city in the world.

Between this region and the Germanic east lies much thicker forest and steeper hills and it is here that you will find Spa, which has given its name to so many thermal spring resorts, and the hand-painted wooden boxes which are once more being produced locally. In winter, the surrounding district is full of skiing enthusiasts, while in the summer it is still a popular holiday resort. There are two great events here during the year: the motor-racing at Francorchamps and the mid-Lent carnival at Stavelot.

The forests of the Ardennes abound with wild deer and boar and in autumn, when the game season is open, most of the local restaurants offer special menus and even gastronomic weekends with game as the main feature.

The region is also a sports centre, especially for water activities. You can canoe along many of the rivers but one of the best organised trips is down the Lesse river from Houyet to Anseremme. If you leave your car at the bottom,

Getting to Know the Country

there is a small train that will take you up to Houyet where you hire your kayak and set off on a journey that will take about four or five hours by the time you have stopped for lunch en route. There are two sets of rapids to be navigated; however, those who prefer not to try can lift their kayaks out of the water and walk them around. Kayaks need to be reserved well in advance as this is an extremely popular activity.

The cliff faces that line some of the river banks in the region and other rock formations provide excellent training grounds for some of the world's best climbers.

For those who prefer a more leisurely activity, there are numerous magnificent castles in the Ardennes to explore (Vêves, Celles and Spontin, the latter now owned by a British couple, and Annevoie, which is also noted for its gardens); the pilgrimage church of Foy-Notre-Dame and the impressive basilica of St Hubert in the town of that name, where hunting animals are brought to be blessed one Sunday in September; the abbeys of Maredsous and Orval, both producing home-brewed beer and their own cheese; as well as the picturesque fortress town of Bouillon. Less attractive, although set in peaceful surroundings, is Hitler's bunker at Brûly-de-Pesche.

It is impossible to ignore the Battle of the Bulge, or, as it is known here, the Battle of the Ardennes. Americans will certainly want to visit Bastogne with its 'Nuts' Museum and the nearby Mardasson memorial. You will find other references to the battle all over the south.

To the west of the French-speaking part of the country is the province of Hainaut. Mons is the capital, a city whose main interest to the tourist is its town hall and Collegiate Church of St Waudru. If you stroke the iron monkey's head which stands in front of the Hôtel de Ville, it is supposed to bring you good luck. There are two annual pageants which take place on the same day in June: the 'Procession of the Golden Carriage', when the statue of St Waudru is somewhat unceremoniously rushed around the cobbled streets; this is followed by the 'Lumeçon', an enactment of the legendary fight between St George and the dragon.

Mons is situated on the Sambre-Meuse coalfield, which also takes in Charleroi. But, when it comes to tourist interest, by far the most appealing town in the province is Tournai. It has a very unusual cathedral with five towers which contains some of Belgium's richest treasures. Tournai was under the rule of England's King Henry VIII for six brief years during which time a citadel was built to house his garrison, the cylindrical keep housing the Military Museum being the only remaining part.

The small town of Binche in Hainaut province is the scene of the most colourful and famous of carnivals in Belgium. It starts on the Sunday before Ash Wednesday and continues until Shrove Tuesday, when the parade of the 'Gilles', a tradition kept within families and passed from father to son, takes place.

The carnival of Binche is not the only important tourist event in this region. Ecaussinnes-Lalaing, which has a fine castle with origins in the twelfth century, holds an unusual event each Whit Monday: a wedding breakfast. Unlike the custom of the Gilles, which began in the fourteenth century, the wedding feast and parade has only been held since 1903. All eligible young men and women can participate in the hope that they will find their marriage partner.

It is impossible to cover all the many attractions of this country in a few words. Virtually every village has its own special event which varies from the grape festival of Overijse to the blessing of the sea at Blankenberge. There is a two-week long beer festival at Wieze each October and a military band parade at Jumet in July. There are air shows and cross-country motorcycle and bicycle races. Village festivals invariably last several days and incorporate all sorts of events, both cultural and social, and there is a lot of eating and drinking and fun for all.

Since Belgium is such a small country and so easily crossed you will be able to go anywhere and return home the same day. However, a long weekend spent visiting a region in detail, or even twenty-four hours away from home makes a pleasant change. Belgian hotels are generally very clean and comfortable no matter what category you select. The system of grading hotels depends on the amenities offered, not on a quality classification.

If you want to be independent and camp either under canvas or in a caravan, there are numerous sites set aside all over the country. They vary as to the type of amenities available and, consequently, the prices they charge.

The Belgian National Tourist Office publishes annually guides giving details of the major events being held in the country, the hotels and the camping sites. Within the country this tourist office is divided into two (although not abroad): the Office de Promotion du Tourisme de la Communauté Française de Belgique (for the French- and German-speaking parts of the country) and the Commissariaat-Generaal voor Toerisme (for the Dutch-speaking part). It has one 'showroom', 3B, at 61 rue des Marché aux Herbes, at the beginning of the Brussels' Ilôt Sacré. Brussels' own tourist office is conveniently placed in the Grand'Place in part of the beautiful Gothic town hall. Every province and town has its own tourist office. In addition, there are some others. However, if you start at the 3B you will certainly be given a good introduction.

Getting To Know Luxembourg

Luxembourg, although only a fraction the size of Belgium, also has much to offer the visitor. Being a much smaller land it is quite natural that it has not the wealth of art treasures. However, it will take you more than a day to really see what the State Museum, in the capital's Fish Market, has to offer.

Another museum to visit is the Musée J.-P. Pescatore which contains a number of seventeenth- to nineteenth-century Dutch and French paintings. But the real sights of the capital are really the almost fairy-tale views to be had across the deep ravines which surround it on three sides, and the magnificent old buildings. The Promenade de la Corniche, a pedestrian walk which follows the seventeenth-century ramparts, provides splendid views. The Bock casemates, some 23km (14 miles) of underground passages created in the eighteenth century, have been used as a refuge in times of war or invasion ever since. They are extremely cold and damp and, therefore, only accessible to the public from Easter to October. The cathedral is mainly Gothic in style but with some Renaissance additions. Visits of the Grand-Ducal Palace are organised in English one day a week. It is only open for guided visits, and details, as well as tickets, must be

Getting to Know the Country

obtained from the city tourist office in the Place d'Armes as the guards outside the entrance have other work to do.

On Easter Monday there is a traditional market, called the E'maischen, held on the Marché aux Poissons. Early risers will be able to buy the much sought-after 'Peckvillercher', a strange bird-whistle made from clay and on which the skilled can play tunes. They have become the collectibles of Luxembourg. Another popular event is the Schobermesse, an enormous amusement fair and market which is held for two weeks at the end of August on the outskirts of the city.

A procession is held on the fifth Sunday after Easter, the Octave of Our Lady of Luxembourg. The national day is celebrated on 23 June.

To the north of the capital lie the forests of the Ardennes and some spectacular scenery. If you take the road out of Luxembourg city in the direction of Echternach you will come to the region known as Little Switzerland because of its resemblance to that other country. Echternach, the principal town of this area, is situated on the Luxembourg bank of the river Sûre, the other side being German. There is a considerable amount of influence from that other country in the architecture of the half-timbered and colour-washed façades of the buildings. The main square rises at an unusually steep angle. This town has a unique dancing procession, which has its origins in the seventh century and honours St Willibrord who cured the 'dance of St Guy'. It takes place on Whit Tuesday and the dancers wend their way through the town, moving to an air that is part polka part march, linked together by white handkerchiefs.

A pretty spot, popular with campers, climbers and walkers, is the small market town of Esch-sur-Sûre, reached after passing through a tunnel in the rocks. The local inn has a large terrace close to the river's edge, which is very popular on sunny afternoons with those looking to quench their thirst. From the *auberge* you can walk up to the enormous dam behind which lies the hydro-electric reservoir of the Lac de la Haute-Sûre. Further along this lake, at Insenborn, there is an important aquatic sports centre offering sailing, canoeing and from where you can bathe.

Getting to Know the Country

Not far from Esch you will come to Wiltz, of especial interest to Americans because of its Battle of the Bulge Museum. But it has other claims to fame in that its picturesque medieval castle, which dominates the surrounding countryside, provides the background for an annual open-air European festival of theatre. An international meeting place for scouts, there are no less than sixteen camping grounds in the area.

You should certainly not miss seeing Clervaux, which is situated on a loop of the River Clerve in a deep, narrow valley, dominated by a large fairly recent, Rhenish-Romanesque style church and a feudal castle. However, the jewel of the north is undoubtedly Vianden, whose origins go back to the ninth century. It is built on the banks of the River Our against a backcloth of wild and rugged scenery. The old ramparts, with watch-towers at strategic points, encircle the town which includes an ancient Trinitarian church, one of the oldest buildings in the country. The house in which Victor Hugo lived during part of his exile from France is now a museum to the poet.

If you drive east from Luxembourg you come to the Moselle valley and the vineyards which provide the excellent white wines that are drunk by the locals as frequently for an aperitif as for an accompaniment to the meal. They have the advantage of being not so sweet as those produced by the Germans from the grapes picked their side of the valley.

You can see the valley from three different ways, by boat, on foot following the water's edge, or by road; each one offers unforgettable views quite different from the others. Whichever you decide on you should not miss taking the road that runs from Wellenstein down the Scheuerberg to Remich, offering some wonderful views of the vineyards and the river far below. Virtually every village has its cellars and you can stop at many of them and try their wines. There are also one or two very good museums which explain the whole process.

Remich is a major crossing point into Germany, a delightful town with a lot of character. It makes a pleasant place to stop on a Sunday and eat fresh trout, washed down with a local wine. Afterwards you can walk along the valley in the direction of Schengen or up towards Ehnen.

Getting to Know the Country

It is at Wasserbillig that the Sûre, which has its source in Belgium, flows into the Moselle. Very much a frontier town, it nevertheless has some points of interest, such as the Gallo-Roman cemetery discovered in the forest close by. The road following the frontier up the Sûre valley to Echternach passes through a completely different type of countryside than that of the flat-bottomed Moselle valley.

South of the capital the country is much flatter and less inspiring than the north and east. It is quite industrial but, nevertheless, there are one or two corners worth visiting. There is the Galgebierg park, ideal for walking and with a game enclosure, educational gardens, roller-skating rink and a camping ground. A more important attraction park is to be found at Bettembourg where children can enjoy a series of animated fairy tales or a number of different sorts of transport, as well as the luna park. Montdorf-les-Bains is likely to appeal more to their parents. It is a pleasant spa town with all the usual amenities and the recently added attraction of a casino.

There are National Tourist Office reception bureaux at the air terminal beside the main station in Luxembourg city and at the airport where you can obtain information on the whole country. Each town has its tourist office and the one for Luxembourg city is in the Place d'Armes.

13
Keeping in Touch with Home

The Belux is so close to Britain that it is not difficult to keep in touch with friends and relatives, London theatres, and life and news in general. In fact, Belgium is closer to Kent than the Midlands. The air flight Brussels–London takes only an hour – and that includes the length of time planes are 'held' awaiting permission to land. And in 1993 we can expect to make the journey by rail between the centre of Brussels and the centre of London in no more than three hours thanks to the Channel tunnel.

There are a number of different ways to regain the shores of Britain and Ireland. Of course, air is generally the quickest means of transport; train and boat or jetfoil, or coach and boat or hovercraft, are other possibilities of group travel, while you can cross with a car, by boat or by hovercraft if you want more independence.

The Belgian national airline, Sabena, operates services from Brussels, Antwerp, Ostend and Liège to London Heathrow, from Brussels to Birmingham, and from Brussels to Manchester. Of the British carriers, there are two major airlines flying into Belgium: British Airways has regular services from Brussels to London Heathrow and Brussels to Manchester; and British Caledonian Airways offers scheduled flights from Brussels and Antwerp to London Gatwick, and from Brussels to Manchester. A Brussels–Birmingham link is operated by British Midland Airways. All these flights offer plenty of opportunity to transfer to domestic routes and, therefore, it is easy to get virtually anywhere in a day.

People travelling to Ireland will find that Aer Lingus has scheduled services from Brussels to Dublin, Cork and Shannon, whilst Sabena operates only into Dublin.

For those heading for the States, both Sabena and Pan Am have been flying between the two countries for years.

Keeping in Touch with Home

At the present time, Sabena serves Boston, New York, Detroit, Chicago and Atlanta direct from Brussels. Pan Am provides daily access out of Brussels to its non-stop flight from London to the principal business centres of the United States, such as New York, Los Angeles, San Francisco, Miami, Washington and Detroit, and, as this goes to press, there is news that the airline may introduce a Brussels–New York direct service in 1987. People's Express has been operating a non-stop link into its New York hub for the last year.

The other method of arriving in the British Isles is by sea. Rail services in Belgium and Britain connect with certain ferries and the jetfoil at Ostend and Dover. Hoverspeed operates a coach and hovercraft connection between Brussels, with a stop at Mons (convenient for SHAPE), and London. A similar service between Amsterdam and London picks up and puts down passengers in Antwerp.

Those travelling with their own vehicle will find that the fastest sea-crossing is between Calais, in France, and Dover. Calais is a little over two hours' drive from central Brussels using the coastal motorway to the border. The hovercraft crosses that stretch of water in approximately thirty-five minutes, while the fastest ferries take about seventy-five minutes. Other services from France into the south-east England ports of Folkestone, Dover and Ramsgate, go from Boulogne and Dunkirk, while there are ferries between Dieppe and Newhaven, Le Havre and Cherbourg and Portsmouth, Cherbourg and the Channel Islands and Weymouth.

The ferry connections between Ireland and France leave from Cork and go to either Roscoff, Le Havre or Cherbourg, or else there is a crossing from Rosslare to Le Havre.

Belgium's ferry ports are Ostend and Zeebrugge from both of which you can sail into Dover. The line is operated by Townsend Thoresen in conjunction with the Belgian Maritime Transport company (RTM/RMT). One other passenger line sails into south-east England, but from Holland: it is Olau's service between Vlissingen (Flushing) and Sheerness.

There are possibilities, too, for those wishing to travel

Keeping in Touch with Home

between Belgium and the Midlands, and farther north without going via Dover. Two ferry companies operate out of Zeebrugge: Townsend Thoresen sails into Felixstowe while North Sea Ferries has a service into Hull. For those who do not mind driving up to Holland, Sealink offers a connection between the Hook of Holland and Harwich, and Olau Line between Rotterdam and Hull.

Anybody importing goods or a car into Belgium or Luxembourg, however, would be advised to use a Belgian port in order to avoid all the paperwork and possible duties involved in either putting the goods into transit before setting out on the journey or declaring them at each frontier.

The post between the Continent and Britain generally travels by air, so there is no need to mark envelopes 'airmail'. In fact, doing so often slows up the distribution process as such correspondence will probably find itself being sorted amongst intercontinental destinations and will lose time in getting back into the European system. This comment is valid for post leaving both Belgium and Britain.

The postal authorities in Belgium are strict on the dimensions and weight of mail, as well as the way it is addressed. In Belgium, the receiver's address should be written on the right-hand side, bottom half of the envelope with the addressee's name on one line, followed by the street and house number in that order on the next line, and the postal code followed by the place name on the line after that. In apartment houses, where there are more than two flats, the letter boxes have to be numbered in order to make delivery easier. These numbers, preceded by 'box' or '*boîte*' (French) or '*bus*' (Dutch), are mentioned after the street number. Thus an address will read:

> Monsieur Jean-Pierre Delvaux
> Boulevard du Souverain 37, boîte 12
> 1170 Bruxelles

When writing abroad, the last line should give the postal code of the destination preceded by the recognised country abbreviation (the same as that used for car registration purposes), which should stand apart in order

Keeping in Touch with Home

to be clear. Thus, an address in London would end:

> Hampstead, London
> GB   NW8 1XT

Return addresses should be indicated, either in the top left-hand corner or on the back, on all communications.

To facilitate automation, envelopes have also been standardised and, failure to use an envelope that conforms to these measurements, at the lowest tariff weight (up to 20g), means that you should stick on double the postage. If you do not put the correct, non-standard amount on the communication will either be returned to you or the excess charged to the receiver. A standard envelope, within the maximum 20g weight, should measure not less than 90×140mm and not more than 120×235mm with a 2mm tolerance. Over 20g and you can send any dimension you like as long as the measurement is not more than a total of 900mm (length, width and depth) and with no side exceeding 600mm. There is also a 2mm tolerance. Limitations exist, too, for other types of post.

The amount you pay depends on the weight of the communication with a maximum weight for letter post of 2kg. Regular postcards go at the minimum letter rate. The maximum weight for parcels is 1kg; above that any parcels must be sent by the railway. There are separate tariffs and weight restrictions for commercial printed matter and non-commercial printed matter.

Should you need to send a document by express delivery, or want to have it registered, you will find that both services carry supplements to the normal cost which consist of (different) one-off prices valid for any destination in Europe.

Residents of houses are required to have a letter box for receiving mail at the beginning of their property, and those numbered apartment building boxes must be placed at the entrance to the building. Post is not delivered to each individual apartment as in Britain. Companies and individuals regularly receiving large quantities of mail will have it delivered separately by van.

Post can be placed in one of the red mail boxes to be

Keeping in Touch with Home

found in the street or it can be delivered to the mail box generally found outside a post office. Collection times are normally indicated on the front of the box. Express mail can be put in a letter box; however, it may not go so fast as if it is handed over the counter in a post office. Registered mail must always be presented at the counter as it has to be recorded. Before handing it over you should ask for a blue form (No 201) on which you indicate the details of the addressee.

Besides the normal postal transactions dealing with the sale of stamps and sending of mail, there is also a giro system operated by the post office. Account numbers are compatible with the banking system and bear numbers starting '000-'. You can use this system rather like a normal bank account except that you will not be provided with a quantity of blank cheques.

Post offices also sell licences to fish on rivers as well as in non-private ponds and lakes. A licence issued for Flanders is not valid for Wallonia, so check the limitations of the licence when purchasing it.

Britons will find that it is easy to pick up the long wave British radio transmissions of Radio Four in Belgium. The BBC World Service, too, is extremely clear and there are two American stations to tune in to: AFN (the American Forces Network) and Radio Free Europe.

The main Belgian radio stations are either in French or Dutch and each language has several stations with broadcasts being put out from other cities as well as Brussels. The BRT (Flemish radio) also puts out an English-language programme on its world service, 'Brussels Calling', which covers events going on in the country, mostly of a cultural nature.

The number of television channels available to Belgian viewers never ceases to surprise Britons coming to the country. Of greatest importance to them is the fact that we can receive BBC1 and BBC2 in most parts of the country, thanks to cable television. Other stations available are the five Belgian ones (BRT1, TV2, RTBF1, Télé 2), the two Dutch ones (Holland 1 and 2), the three French ones (TF1, Antenne 2, France 3), RTL (Radio-Television Luxembourg), three German channels (Germany 1, 2 and 3) and two for which you need to take out a special

Keeping in Touch with Home

subscription (Sky Channel and Music Box). There are some stations, too, which cannot be picked up all over the country: TV5 (a French/Swiss/Canadian channel), RAI (Italian), RTL-Plus (German channel) and a number of local televisions. Since most of the Dutch-language stations (that is, including the BRT channels) regularly show English and American films in the original language and, to a lesser degree, documentaries, there is plenty of choice in addition to the BBC programmes.

It is possible to buy English-language newspapers and magazines not just in the centre of the large cities but also in residential areas where there are major concentrations of English-speaking people living. British newspapers are particularly expensive but can be obtained in the centre of Brussels before midday on the day of publication. Americans can obtain the *International Herald Tribune*, which is published in France, and the European edition of the *Wall Street Journal*, which has its offices in Brussels, locally and the morning of publication.

There is one English-speaking magazine, *The Bulletin*, and one new newspaper, *The Belgian Weekly Gazette*, in Belgium. Both are weeklies. *The Bulletin*'s main aim is to inform it readership about Belgian news and happenings in general, as well as including some news on community activities. *The Gazette* has set out to give more news of community interest.

Specifically About Luxembourg

Air transportation is more important in Luxembourg if you are wanting to head back to Britain for a weekend than it is for people living in Belgium, since a car journey would mostly necessitate travelling through a Belgian port and you must drive across the whole country to get there. Luxembourg has regular air links both through Luxair and British Airways with London. There are good services, too, with the United States and Icelandair regularly offers advantageous prices.

While the postal services are basically the same in Luxembourg as in Belgium, they are mostly cheaper. The method of addressing is slightly different, however, in that in Luxembourg the street number is put before the name of the road.

Keeping in Touch with Home

As far as radio programmes are concerned, the RTL broadcasts an English-language community programme from Monday to Saturday during the afternoon. AFN and BBC world programmes can be picked up easily, too. Television, however, is restricted to the two RTL stations, the three German and three French stations, and the two RTBF channels. The BBC cannot be captured at the moment.

The arrival of British newspapers is largely dependent on the weather since they are flown in. The two European editions of the American press come in by train and so usually arrive on time.

There is a small English-language, weekly newspaper, the *Luxembourg News Digest*, which contains some news on local happenings and information of interest to the communities.

14
To Stay On or to Leave

As you come to the end of your stay in Belgium you will probably start to look around you and to realise what you are going to miss if you do return home – the beautiful Ardennes, the sandy beaches at the coast, the marvellous motorway system, the short journey to work, the school bus service, your home help, the good friends you have made, and those delicious meals out and the fattening but gorgeous chocolates. You may not agree with all of these suggestions but I am sure there is more than one item in that list that you are going to miss, and you will probably add a few more.

Have you been to Bruges? Have you managed to see the Ommegang in Brussels? And have you visited the Church of St Leonard in Zoutleeuw? If you have not done half of the things you wanted to whilst you were here you will have many regrets.

Perhaps you will not have time to think of these things before you go. Every year one hears of somebody recalled suddenly owing to an unexpected promotion or a reshuffle within the head office. If you have only a few days' notice to move on then you will not think of these things probably until you are in your new home.

Of course, returning home can have its advantages. Perhaps the children are at boarding school there and it will be nice for the family to be closer together. Or maybe your parents are showing signs of the passing years and you would like to be nearer to help. Those people who are not able to adapt to driving on the right side of the road and therefore prefer not to drive at all miss having the independence that a car provides. And there are others who find trying to learn a foreign language difficult and would be happier in a country which is English-speaking. Or perhaps you have never really settled in here and you

To Stay On or to Leave

are longing to get back to your friends and family, and Rose's Lime Juice with your gin.

If you do have the chance to stay on, you will have to give the opportunity some serious thought. It may be that your children are at school here and that it is the wrong time to move them. Or the possibility of going back could just fall at the right time to transfer them to a school back home. The chances are that, if you came out on a fixed contract, your home will be free for you to move back into, but if it is rented for another year or so what will it be like to move back and to live in somebody else's property in the meantime? And, if you stay longer, will you be eligible for the same tax concessions as you may have been enjoying?

Single people might prefer to return to the social set they once moved in if they have not made many friends here. Certainly the great disadvantage in being a foreigner in another country is that you tend to make and lose friends more easily as they come and go internationally; and people on their own are more free to move on than couples or families.

But one thing you should be aware of – and it is worse the longer you have lived away from your homeland – is that going back can be just as hard as moving to a strange country. It is culture shock in reverse, called 're-entry' by the Americans. Time has not stood still whilst you were away and, no matter how much of the newspapers you have read, things will have changed that you do not know about. There is no way you can pick up your old life just where you left off. As you did on arrival here, you will start comparing everything with the previous home and, if you are not careful, your friends and family will soon become bored with hearing 'In Belgium . . .' and resent your criticism of their lives.

Let us consider for a moment that the decision is made and that you are leaving Belgium, either voluntarily or involuntarily. Virtually all those steps you had to take to come have to be taken again in order to go home. One of the first things to do is to send a registered letter to your landlord terminating your lease. You will need to arrange for a removal company to pack and transport your belongings. The various utilities (gas, electricity, water and telephone) need to be informed and arrangements

To Stay On or to Leave

made to read the relevant meters and cut off each service. The local income tax department must be informed and a request made to close your file. Other people you will need to notify are children's schools, insurance companies, the mutuality and banks, although you may prefer to leave an account open for a little time after your departure at least. The local police and the commune will also need to be told and, when all is finalised, you must return your identity card to the town hall.

At some stage you should go to the embassy of the country to which you are moving to find out what steps must be taken to smooth the way. And, if you are moving to another foreign country, write to the publisher of this book to see if there is a book in the *Long Stays* series to help you settle in.

In between all these jobs, you will probably want to rush out and buy some souvenirs to take back for yourself and for friends. Belgian linen will fit easily into a suitcase as will local lace. One of the best guarantees that such products were genuinely made in this country is the quality control mark that they bear. You could also buy from a reliable supplier. There is much imitation machine-made lace coming in from abroad.

Belgium has played a considerable part in the raising of ceramics to an art form, with many of the country's artists having been directly or indirectly influenced by Bernard Leech. You may have started a collection while you were here and want to add a few more pieces to it before leaving.

Pewter-ware, which generally comes from the Meuse valley, is also typical of the country. Large pewter plates are often used in restaurants as an under dish to keep those you eat off warm, a habit which looks particularly attractive on a refectory or oak table.

It would not be possible to make suggestions for souvenirs to take home without mentioning the local crystal made by the famous Val St Lambert factory. The old traditional styles, in which coloured glass plays an important part, make lasting souvenirs, and a newer, more commercial range is ideal for less expensive giving.

One of the Toone-type rod puppets makes an unusual decoration and will evoke memories of sitting cramped in the tiny theatre, probably not understanding every word because the show is given in the Brussels dialect, but enjoying the atmosphere. Puppets that are not authentic can be bought all over the country, but, if you want a real Toone marionette that will set you back several thousand francs as they are greatly sought after at home and abroad.

Jewellery is another creative art which is very well developed in Belgium but which is not particularly cheap and, of course, it is in Antwerp that 47 per cent of the world's diamond consumption is polished. The town has even given its name to a special cut which shows off the stone far better than the old traditional method.

Another important product Belgium makes is sports equipment, especially tennis rackets in which it leads the world. No tennis player will want to leave before renewing his rackets. And, of course, it is traditionally a major centre for producing guns and rifles which are mostly made by Browning in Liège.

Perhaps, however, you have decided to stay on. You will inevitably start to put down roots and settle in more to the community. Perhaps your lease is up for renewal and you can take advantage of the fact to move to other premises. When going through all the procedures of changing over from one home to another, you will have to go through all the steps mentioned above at both communes if you are changing areas. Whatever happens, you should not forget to notify the police, especially if you have a car. It is one of the easiest things to overlook and failure to notify the change of a car's domicile to the police will result in a fine when they eventually discover the omission.

Specifically About Luxembourg

When looking for something to take back as a reminder of your stay in Luxembourg, you could buy one of the cast-iron miniature firebacks, called 'taak', which are made at the Fonderie de Mersch. Among the vast choice of porcelain and ceramics produced by Villeroy & Boch, there is a range of decorative plates depicting various landscapes around the Grand Duchy.

Appendix 1
Relevant Addresses

(*Where an address is given with an alternative, the first is the French-speaking organisation and the second the Flemish group.*)

Belgian Customs Office
Ministère des Finances
Direction Générale des Douanes, Boulevard du Jardin Botanique 50, 1000 Bruxelles

or

Ministerie van Financiën
Algemene Direktie der Douanen, Kruidtuinlaan 50, 1000 Brussel

Car Registration
Ministry of Communications
Direction B2, Cantersteen 12, 1000 Brussels

Chambers of Commerce
American Chamber of Commerce in Belgium
Avenue des Arts 50, box 5, 1040 Brussels

British Chamber of Commerce in Belgium & Luxembourg
Britannia House, Rue Joseph II 30, 1040 Brussels

Church Services in English
Anglican
Holy Trinity Pro-Cathedral (Anglican/Episcopal)
Rue Capitaine Crespel 29, 1050 Brussels

All Saints Church (Anglican/Episcopal)
Chaussée de Louvain 563, 1328 Ohain

St Boniface Church
Grétrystraat 39, 2000 Antwerp

Anglican Church
Quai Marcellis 21, 4000 Liège

Assembly of God
The Christian Center
Drève des Chasseurs 27, 1410 Waterloo

Appendix 1: Relevant Addresses

Christian Scientist
Church of Christ
Chaussée de Vleurgat 96, 1050 Brussels

Church of Christ
Rue Lamarck 28, 4000 Liège

International Baptist Church
Rue J. Hoton 17, 1200 Brussels

Jewish
Brussels Synagogue
Rue de la Régence 32, 1000 Brussels

Communauté Israelite de Schaerbeek
Rue Rogier 126, 1030 Brussels

Communauté Israelite Liberale de Belgique
Avenue Kersbeek 96-98, 1190 Brussels

Communauté Israelite Orthodoxe
Rue de la Clinique 67a, 1070 Brussels

Lutheran
The American Lutheran Church
Avenue Salomé 7, 1200 Brussels

The Danish Lutheran Church
Avenue Delleur 31-33, 1170 Brussels

The Norwegian Church in Brussels
Chemin du Bon Dieu 47, 1410 Waterloo

Mormon
Church of Christ of the Latter-day Saints
Avenue de Bruxelles 1000, 1820 Strombeek-Bever

Church of Christ of the Latter-day Saints
Avenue de la Grande Rotisse 61, 4030 Grivegnée

Presbyterian
St Andrew's Church of Scotland
Chaussée de Vleurgat 181, 1050 Brussels

Protestant
The American Protestant Church
ISB campus, Kattenberg 19, 1170 Brussels

The United Protestant Church of Belgium
Rue du Champ de Mars 5, 1050 Brussels

The American Protestant Church in Antwerp
Noorderlaan 169, 2000 Antwerp

Appendix 1: Relevant Addresses

Quaker
The Religious Society of Friends
Square Ambiorix 50, 1040 Brussels

Roman Catholic
Our Lady of Mercy Parish
St Anne's Church, Place de la Sainte Alliance 10, 1180 Brussels

St Anthony's Parish
Avenue des Anciens Combattants 23-25, 1950 Kraainem

St Joseph's Church
Rue Belliard 28, 1040 Brussels

St Nicholas's Church
Rue de Tabora 6, 1000 Brussels

Heilig Hart Instituut
Lamorinièrestraat 150, 2018 Antwerp

Couvent des Dominicains
Quai Mative 38, 4000 Liège

Common Market Special Employment Service
Manpower Services Commission
Sedoc Section, Employment Service Division, Overseas Placing Unit, Moorfoot, Sheffield S1 4PQ

Community Associations and Clubs
American-Belgian Association
Rue Bréderode 13, 1000 Brussels

American Belgian Association in Antwerp, clubhouse
Venusstraat 17, 2000 Antwerp

American Club of Antwerp
Venusstraat 17, 2000 Antwerp

American Club of Brussels
Sheraton Hotel, Place Rogier, 1210 Brussels

Belgo-British Union
Rue Bréderode 13, 1000 Brussels

Brussels British Community Association
Rue L. Hymans 20, 1060 Brussels

Driving
For information on the driving test, schools and testing centres contact:

Groupement des Organismes de Contrôle Automobile
Rue de la Loi 34, 1040 Bruxelles

or

Appendix 1: Relevant Addresses

Groepering van Organismen voor de Controle van Automobielen
Wetstraat 34, 1040 Brussels

Embassies
British Embassy
Britannia House, Rue Joseph II 28, 1040 Brussels

United States Embassy
Boulevard du Régent 27, 1000 Brussels

Belgian Embassy
103 Eaton Square, London SW1 9AB

Firearms and Weapons Licence
Gouvernment Provincial du Brabant
Rue du Chêne 22, 1000 Bruxelles

or

Provinciebestuur van Brabant
Eikstraat 22, 1000 Brussel

Help Service
Community Help Service
Rue St-Georges 102, bte 20, 1050 Brussels

Higher Education
Art Studies:
Ecole Nationale Supérieure des Arts Visuels de la Cambre
Abbaye de la Cambre 21, 1050 Brussels

Modern dance/ballet school:
Mudra asbl
Rue Bara 103, 1070 Brussels

Libraries
British Council Library
Rue Joseph II, 30, 1040 Brussels

American Library
Square du Bastion 1c, 1050 Brussels

Children's Library housed in the
Centre Crousse, Rue au Bois 11, 1150 Brussels

Meat, English and American Cuts
Eddy's Meat Market
Rue de l'Elan 62-64, 1170 Brussels

Newspapers and Magazines
English
The Bulletin
Ackroyd Publications sa, Avenue Molière 329, 1060 Brussels

Appendix 1: Relevant Addresses

The Belgian Weekly Gazette
Avenue F. Roosevelt 142, 1050 Brussels

Living in Belgium & Luxembourg
Chaussée de Waterloo 878, 1180 Brussels

Flemish
De Standaard
Alfons Gossetlaan 30A, 1720 Groot-Bijgaarden

Het Laatste Nieuws
E. Jacqmainlaan 105, 1000 Brussels

French
Le Soir
Place de Louvain 21, 1000 Brussels

Professional Card
Service de la Carte Professionnelle
Ministère des Classes Moyennes, World Trade Center, Tour 2, Boulevard E. Jacqmain 162, bte 54, 1000 Bruxelles

or

Beroepskaart Dienst
Ministerie van Middenstand, World Trade Center, Toren 2, E. Jacqmainlaan 162, bus 54, 1000 Brussel

Radio and Television Licences
Radio et Télévision Redevances
Boulevard Emile Jacqmain 164, 1000 Bruxelles

or

Kijk- en Luistergeld
Emile Jacqmainlaan 164, 1000 Brussels

Schools Mentioned
English-speaking in and around Brussels
British Primary School
Stationstraat 6, 1982 Vossem

British School of Brussels
Steenweg op Leuven 15b, 1980 Tervuren

Brussels American School
John F. Kennedylaan 12, 1960 Sterrebeek

Brussels Christian School
Rue Profonde 100, 1970 Wezembeek-Oppem

Brussels English Primary School
Avenue Franklin Roosevelt 23, 1050 Brussels

European School (Brussels I)
Avenue du Vert Chasseur 46, 1180 Brussels

Appendix 1: Relevant Addresses

European School (Brussels II)
Avenue Oscar Jespers 75, 1200 Brussels

International Christian Academy
Drève des Chasseurs 27, 1410 Waterloo

International School of Brussels
Kattenberg 19, 1170 Brussels

St John's International School
Drève Richelle 146, 1410 Waterloo

English-speaking in and around Antwerp
Antwerp English Primary School and Kindergarten
Lange Lozanastraat 238, 2018 Antwerp

Antwerp International School
Veltwijcklaan 180, 2070 Ekeren

E.E.C. School
Jacob Jordaenstraat 77-81, 2000 Antwerp

English-speaking close to Liège
International School of Liège
Rue Pierre Henvard 64, 4920 Embourg-Chaudfontaine

English-speaking in Mol
European School of Mol
Europawijk 100, 2400 Mol

English-speaking at SHAPE
SHAPE International School
7010 SHAPE

Other Foreign Schools
Deutsche Schule Brüssel
Lange Eikstraat 71, 1970 Wezembeek-Oppem

Ecole Japonaise de Bruxelles
Avenue des Meuniers 133, 1160 Brussels

Ecole Reine Astrid
Chaussée de Waterloo 280, 1640 Rhode-St-Genèse

Lycée Français de Belgique
Avenue du Lycée Français 9, 1180 Brussels

Lycée d'Anvers/Collège Marie-José
Isabellalei 131, 2018 Antwerp

Nederlandse School, Prinses Juliana
Rue d'Oultremont 19, 1040 Brussels

Belgian Schools Mentioned in this Book
Ecole Hamaïde

Appendix 1: Relevant Addresses

Avenue Hamoir 31, 1190 Brussels

Ecole Internationale 'Le Verseau'
Rue de Wavre 60, 1301 Bierges

Shooting Licences
Commissariats d'Arrondissements
Avenue de Jette 120, 1090 Bruxelles

or

Arrondissementscommissariaten van Brussel
Jettelaan 120, 1090 Brussel

Theory Test
Administration des Eaux et Forêts
Chaussée d'Ixelles 31, 1050 Bruxelles

or

Bestuur van Waters en Bossen
Steenweg op Elsene 31, 1050 Brussel

Social Security (British)
The Overseas Office
Department of Health & Social Security, Newcastle-upon-Tyne, NE98 1YX

Specialist French Courses in Brussels
Institut de Phonetique
Université Libre de Bruxelles – CP 110, Avenue Paul Héger – Préf 1, 1050 Brussels

Centre de Phonetique Appliquée
Avenue Louise 412, 1050 Brussels

Institut de Formation de Cadres pour le Developement (IFCAD)
Avenue Legrand 57-59, 1050 Brussels

Ecole Pratique de l'Alliance Française
Place Quételet 6, 1030 Brussels

Cours de Langues Vivantes
Chambre de Commerce de Bruxelles, Avenue Louise 500, 1050 Brussels

Ecole Technique Supérieure de l'Etat
Boulevard Bischoffsheim 5, 1000 Bruxelles

'Cours Pratiques de Langues Vivantes'
Athénée Robert Catteau, Rue Ernest Allard 49, 1000 Brussels

Telephone (Central Office)
Régie des Télégraphes et Téléphones
Tour RTT, Boulevard E. Jacqmain 164, 1000 Brussels

Appendix 1: Relevant Addresses

or

Regie van Telegrafie en Telefonie RTT
E. Jacqmainlaan 164, 1000 Brussels

Tourist Offices
Commissariat General au Tourisme de Belgique
Rue Marché-aux-Herbes 61, 1000 Brussels

or

Commissariaat Generaal voor Toerisme
Grasmarkt 61, 1000 Brussels

Tourist Information Brussels
Hôtel de Ville, Grand'Place, 1000 Brussels

Belgian Tourist Office
38 Dover Street, London W1X 3RB

Belgian Tourist Office
745 Fifth Avenue, New York NY 10151

Universities
Applications departments at Belgian universities which have a comparatively large number of English-speaking students.

French-speaking
Bureau des Equivalences
Service des Inscriptions – CP 176
Bâtiment A, Université Libre de Bruxelles, Avenue F. Roosevelt 50, 1050 Brussels

Director of Admissions, Université Catholique de Louvain
Place de l'Université 1, 1348 Louvain-la-Neuve

Dutch-speaking
Dienst Inschrijvingen, Vrije Universiteit Brussel
Pleinlaan 2, 1050 Brussels

Dienst Inschrijvingen, Katholieke Universiteit Leuven
3000 Leuven

English-language Graduate Courses
College of Europe
Dijver 10-11, 8000 Bruges

Boston University
Avenue de la Toison d'Or 17a box 69, 1060 Brussels

Open University (UK)
Bôite Postale 18, Schaerbeek 8 (Place Dailly), 1030 Brussels

Water (in Brussels)
Compagnie Intercommunale Bruxelloise des Eaux
Rue aux Laines 70, 1000 Bruxelles

Appendix 1: Relevant Addresses

or

Brussels Intercommunale Watermaatschappij
Wolstraat 70, 1000 Brussel

Women's Clubs
American Women's Club,
Avenue des Erables 1, 1640 Rhode-St-Genèse

British & Commonwealth Women's Club
Luxor Park 16, 1160 Brussels

Specifically About Luxembourg

Authorisation de Séjour
Police des Etrangers at the Ministère de la Justice
16 boulevard Royal, Luxembourg

Church Services in English
Anglican Episcopal
Konvikt Chapel, 5 Avenue Marie-Thérèse, Luxembourg

Evangelical
Christian Community Church
11 Boulevard Pierre Dupong, Merl/Belair

Mormon
Church of Jesus Christ of Latter-day Saints
11 Rue Adolphe Fischer, Luxembourg

Roman Catholic
Church of St Alphonse
Rue des Capucins, Luxembourg

Church of Sts Pierre et Paul
Hollerich

Sacré-Coeur Chapel
5 Avenue Marie-Thérèse, Luxembourg

Driving Licence
Ministry of Transport
Bureau des Permis de Conduire, 23 boulevard Royal, Luxembourg

Electricity, Outside Luxembourg City
CEGEDEL
rue Thomas Edison, 1445 Strassen

Embassies
American Embassy
22 boulevard Emmanuel Servais, 2535 Luxembourg

British Embassy
boulevard Royal 28, Luxembourg City

Appendix 1: Relevant Addresses

Luxembourg Embassy
27 Wilton Crescent, London SW1X 8SD

Fishing Licence
Commissariat de District
34 avenue de la Porte-Neuve, Luxembourg

Gas, Electricity and Water for Luxembourg City
Recette Communale
51 boulevard Royal, Luxembourg

Hunting Licence
Administration des Eaux et Forêts
34 avenue de la Porte-Neuve, Luxembourg

Libraries
British Library
44 Rue de Strasbourg, Luxembourg

Miami University Library
45 Avenue Monterey, Luxembourg

Motoring Club
Automobile Club of Luxembourg
Résidence Belle Isle, 13 route de Longwy, Helfenterbrück

Newspapers
Luxembourg News Digest
34 avenue Victor Hugo, Limpertsberg, 1750 Luxembourg

Schools (for foreigners)
American International School of Luxembourg
188 avenue de la Faïencerie, 1511 Luxembourg

European School
Boulevard Konrad Adenauer, Luxembourg-Kirchberg

Telephone Connections
PTT, Bureau 110, Division Technique, 17 rue de Hollerich, BP 1506, 1015 Luxembourg

Tourist Offices
Luxembourg Trade & Tourist Office
36 Piccadilly, London W1

Ville de Luxembourg
Place d'Armes, BP 181, 2011 Luxembourg

Welcome/Help Service
Administration Communale
Ville de Luxembourg, 9 rue Chimay (Petit Passage), Luxembourg

Women's Clubs
American Women's Club
BP 2341, Luxembourg Gare

Appendix 2
Glossary

English	French	Dutch
Accommodation		
apartment	appartement	appartement
auction	vente publique	openbare verkoping
'Basic Rule'	acte de base	basieakte
estate agent	agent immobilier	makelaar in onroerende goederen
for sale	à vendre	te koop
furnished	meublé	gemeubeld
house	maison	huis
lease	bail	huurkontrakt
private sale	de gré à gré	uit de hand
rent	loyer	huur
solicitor	notaire	notaris
to rent	à louer	te huur
unfurnished	non meublé	niet gemeubeld
Banking and Business		
current account	compte à vue	zichtrekening
deposit account	carnet de dépôt	depositoboekje
income tax	impôts	belasting
insurance	assurance	verzekering
loan	prêt	lening
tax return	déclaration	aangifte
Value Added Tax	TVA	BTW
'virement'	virement	overschrijving
Driving		
provision or deductible	franchise	vrijstelling
registration card or log book	carte d'immatriculation	inschrijvingsbewijs
special 'fine' stamps	amende	borterzegels

Appendix 2: Glossary

English	French	Dutch
Food and Food Shops		
bakery	boulangerie	bakkerij
butcher's	boucherie	beenhouwerij
butcher's selling cooked meats	charcuterie	fijne vleeswaren
cake shops	pâtisseries	pasteibakkerijen
dish of the day	plat du jour	dagschotel
horsemeat butcher's	boucherie chevaline	slager-paardevlees
menu of the day	menu du jour	dagmenu
muttonmeat butcher's	moutonnerie	slagers-schapevlees
grocer's shop	épicerie	kruidenierswinkel
Health		
appointment	rendez-vous	afspraak
chemist	pharmacie	apotheek
medicine	médicament	geneesmiddel
sickness funds	mutuelles	ziekenfonds
In the Home		
do-it-yourself	bricolage	brico
heating oil	mazout	stookolie
Official Documents		
certificate of good conduct and morality	Certificat de Bonne Vie et Moeurs	Bewijs van goed gedrag en zeden
identity card	carte d'identité	identiteitskaart
professional card	carte professionnelle	beroepskaart
town hall	maison communale	gemeentehuis
work permit	permis de travail	arbeidstoelating
Schools		
commune school	école communale	gemeenteschool
liberal school	école libre	vrije school
nursery school	gardienne	kleuterschool
professional school	école professionnelle	beroepsopleiding
provincial school	école provinciale	provincialeschool
state school	école d'état	staatsschool
Shops		
barber	coiffeur pour hommes	herenkapper
dry cleaner's	teinturerie	droogskuis

191

Appendix 2: Glossary

English	French	Dutch
hairdresser	coiffeur	kapper
laundry	blanchisserie	wasserij

Telephone Books
'Yellow Pages' Pages d'Or Gouden Gids

Specifically About Luxembourg

Local council	commune
Town hall	mairie

Further Reading

American Chamber of Commerce in Belgium: *The AmCham Directory.*
(An annual publication, this is the chamber's official list of American companies in Belgium and its membership directory. In addition to listing companies in various ways — by Belgian province, US state, etc — it also incorporates information on the American Chambers of Commerce worldwide and some basic material on doing business in the United States, in Belgium and in the EC.)

American Chamber of Commerce in Belgium: *Doing business in Belgium: a practical information guide for the foreign businessman.*
(The current edition of this sixty-page booklet was printed in March 1984 but a considerable amount of the information contained is still relevant. It is hoped to revise the work during the course of 1987.)

British Chamber of Commerce for Belgium and Luxembourg: *Year Book.*
(This is the annual listing of the Chamber's members.)

Carson, Patricia. *The Fair Face of Flanders*, published by E. Story-Scientia.
(A well-written historical book on the Flemish people.)

Community Help Service: *The Children's Guide to Brussels (and all around it!).*
(This is a delightfully produced guide designed to help parents occupy their children usefully.)

Fonds Mercator: *Flemish Art From the Beginning till Now.*
(A beautiful, informative book that will grace any coffee table and give the newcomer a good understanding of one of the richest artistic heritages in the world.)

Frommer, Arthur. *A Masterpiece Called Belgium*, prepared for Sabena Belgian World Airlines.
(This is a very good guide for somebody spending a day or two in

Further Reading

Belgium in that it gives a real insight into the country but, from the point of view of being a guidebook, covers only the major places and monuments that such a visitor will have time to see. Published in 1984, however, the prices must now be used only as a guideline.)

Gordon, Enid, and Shirley, Midge. *A Taste of the Belgian Provinces*, published by the Tuesday Group.
(An attractive work more suited to the drawing-room, with its sepia prints of Belgian life of yesteryear, than to the kitchen. A historical document, it includes recipes for certain ingredients no longer available, such as thrushes, and others extremely hard to come by, such as woodcock.

Hazelton, Nika. *The Belgian Cook Book*, published by Atheneum.
(This work first appeared in 1970 and, as about half of the volume is given over to tourism and life in the country, there have obviously been changes at some of the restaurants mentioned. The recipes given are, presumably, adapted for the American market in that preparations for venison or wild boar are omitted (both great delicacies of the Belgian cuisine) and only one recipe each is given for rabbit and hare, which are regularly served in numerous ways.)

Insight Publications sa: *Living in Belgium & Luxembourg*.
(An annual guide which gives actual pricing or indications for all aspects of life in the country, including such services as telephone, water, electricity and transport. It also contains detailed information on all the foreign schools, including the basic cost of education at each. Besides giving a brief background to the country (history, geography and the political scene) the guide provides up-to-date directories of useful names, addresses and telephone numbers (everything from embassies to the English-speaking community's clubs) in four cities: Brussels, Antwerp, Liège and Luxembourg. There are sections on leisure activities both within the foreign community and throughout the country.)

Keyes, Roger. *Outrageous Fortune*, published by Secker & Warburg.
(Subtitled *The Tragedy of Leopold III of the Belgians, 1901–1941*, the work has provoked a certain amount of criticism especially for the way it portrays various leading statesmen of the period. A second volume is planned to continue the biography up until the king's death in 1983.)

Laconti: *Brussels Seen by Naïf Artists*.
(A delightful volume with an English text considered far superior to that of the French version.)

Further Reading

Luxembourg City Tourist Office: *A Walk Through the Green Heart of Europe.*
(This small pamphlet takes the visitor on two walks through the capital visiting all the major sights.)

Luxembourg National Tourist Office: *Grand Duchy of Luxembourg.*
(A thirty-two-page booklet giving information on all there is to see and do in the country and facts of interest to the tourists.)

Mann, Michael. *And They Rode One,* published by Michael Russell.
(A slim volume which explains well the Battle of Waterloo.)

Merckx: *Belgium.*
(There are two versions, a short and a longer edition, of this primarily pictorial work with captions in four languages — English, French, Dutch and German. Both make good souvenirs.

Tomes, John. *Belgium & Luxembourg,* published by Ernest Benn Limited.
(One of the Blue Guide series, this book offers about the best value for money on the market and virtually covers every kilometre of the two countries. Out of print at the time of this writing, it is due for reprinting in February 1987.)

Tourist Information Brussels (TIB): *Brussels, guide and map . . .*
(A complete guide for the tourist visiting Brussels covering the history, attractions and practical information on being a tourist in Belgium. All the museums are listed with a short explanation of what each contains but, more importantly, the opening hours and how to get there by public transport. It is updated annually.)

Tourist Information Brussels (TIB): *Gourmet.*
(A listing of restaurants which are members of the tourist office of Brussels and are situated either in the city or on the outskirts. A jury of well-known critics awards annually 'iris' symbols to those they consider deserve the accolade (the iris being the flower of Brussels).)

Tugendhat, Christopher. *Making Sense of Europe,* published by Viking.
(The Common Market explained by someone who really knows all about it having served as a Commissioner at the EEC.)

Van Isacker, Karel, and Van Uyten, Raymond. *Antwerp. Twelve Centuries of History and Culture,* published by Fonds Mercator.
(An attractive work that will make a good souvenir for any resident or visitor to the city.)

Acknowledgements

Even though I had to go through many of the procedures outlined in this book when I first came to Belgium over twenty years ago, it is obvious that such a work could not have been written without reference to a number of people who are experts in their various fields.

Both the staffs of the Belgian and the Luxembourg embassies in London went to great lengths to assist me in compiling the section on the legal requirements needed to take up residence. My special thanks go to the Belgian Chargé d'Affaires, Mr Charles Raulier, Mrs Prima, and Messrs Bauwens, Dewulf and Schoup, and to Mr Cape and Miss Ansell at the Luxembourg embassy. My Luxembourg research advanced rapidly and effectively with the help of Messrs André Claude and T. Pescatore at the Government's information and press service, and that of Mr Henri Neyen and Miss Koders in the city's Foreigner's Welcome Office. I have also received valuable assistance from Miss Susan White at the British Embassy and Mr Michael Barry, Mrs Laplume and Messrs Floren and Gaul at the American Embassy in Luxembourg.

Mr and Mrs J. White of Canterbury Property Management, who handle property for a large number of expatriates, provided invaluable advice concerning the inevitable problem of what to do with one's own home when leaving Britain. On the Belgian side, Mrs 'Rusti' Kile and Mrs Jacqueline Moens de Fernig both contributed to the local property market section and the responsibilities of landlord and tenant. Mr Roger Brosius, of Arthur Pierre, explained the latest changes in the importing of goods, and especially cars and provided additional information on removals to and from the Belux.

I am grateful to many people for their remarks and comments on being a foreigner here and what day-to-day living is like but particularly to Mrs Minda Alexander, Mrs Vivien Herbert, and Miss Hannelore Köhring. Mrs Bonnie Ham and Miss Eileen McQueen, both residents of Luxembourg for some years, were kind enough to allow me to draw from their experiences of life in that country.

For the work and business chapter I received especial help from Mr Robert A. Gattie of Tasa on finding executive employment, and Multi-Consult, the Belgian member company of

Acknowledgements

Deloitte Haskins & Sells International, for the income tax regulations.

Mr Robert F. Schaecher, headmaster of the Antwerp International School, and Miss Fiona Dunnachie who works in that institution's pre-school unit, provided useful comment on the schooling section.

Dr Herman Willems of Overijse gave invaluable assistance with the medical information, and I am very grateful to Professor P. Ide and his team at Louvain University Hospital for their important contribution.

Mrs Cecile Pierrard and Mrs Elisabeth Puttart in Belgium, Mr Pierre Claus at the Belgian Tourist Office in London, Mr Hausemer and Mrs Schoup in Luxembourg, and Mr Serge Moes at the Luxembourg Tourist Office in London all helped with information on tourism and gastronomy. I am also indebted to the Belgian Tourist Office and the Luxembourg National Tourist Office for supplying the photographs which illustrate this book.

I am grateful to the staff of the Strathmore Bookshop near Woluwé Shopping Center for their help in compiling a list for further reading.

A special thank you goes to two colleagues who followed this work from beginning to end: Mrs Anne Devreux and Mrs Sheila Chabeau.

Finally, I offer a big thank you to my husband, Fernand Ducastel. Not only did he put his expert eye over the insurance sections, but he also supported and encouraged me in hundreds of small ways, with never a word of complaint when meals were served late or I vanished to the study weekend after weekend, during the not always easy gestation period of the book.

Carole Hazlewood
Overijse, Belgium

Index

Abbeys: Maredsous, 128, 163
  Orval, 163
  Villers-la-Ville, 161
Accommodation, 52–66
  Furniture tax, 61
  In Belgium, 52–64, 69
  In Luxembourg, 64–6
  Temporary, 19, 79
Air Transport, 169–170, 174
Ambulances, 106, 107
Animals, 13
  Health certificate, 13
  Vaccination, 13
Antiques, 76–7
Antwerp (Antwerpen), 9, 19, 157–8, 169, 170
Ardennes, 9, 10, 29, 131, 161–3
Ardennes, Battle of, 163

Baker's, 129
Ballet, 120, 124
Banking, 40–3, 51
  Accounts, 18, 41
  Eurocheques, 41–2
  Postal giro, 43, 173
  Standing orders, 42
  Statements, 42
  Transfers, 41
Baptism, 29
Bastogne, 163
Beer, 27, 128, 163
Belgo-Luxembourg Economic Union, 9
Belux, 8, 33
Bettembourg, 168
Blankenberge, 164

Bokrijk, 159
Bouillon, 163
Brabant, 159, 160
Bruges (Brugge), 9, 154–5, 176
Brûly-de-Pesche, 163
Brussels (Bruxelles/Brussel), 9, 19, 22–3, 159–161, 169, 170
Bulge, Battle of, 163, 167
Bus, 149, 150, 152
Butchers, 130–2, 139

Camping/caravan sites, 164–5, 168
Carpets, 77, 84
Car: Buying a, 140
  Importing a, 143–4
  Leasing a, 143
  Number plate, 142
  Registration, 141, 151, 180
  Road tax, 142, 151
  Technical Control, 144, 151
Carnivals: Binche, 164
  Eupen, 162
  Stavelot, 162
Casino, 154, 168
Castles: Aigremont, 161
  Annevoie, 163
  Celles, 163
  Franc-Waret, 161
  Jehay-Bodegnée, 161
  Spontin, 163
  Vêves, 163
Central heating, 69
  Oil-fired, 72
Ceramics, 178, 179

Chambers of commerce, 33, 47, 115, 180
Charities, 116–19
Charleroi, 163
Cheese, 128, 133, 163
Chemists, 103–4, 107, 134
Chicory, 127–128
Children's activities, 114–16, 120, 123
Choirs, 113
Christian names, use of, 24, 31
Churches, 112, 119–120, 123, 180–3, 192–3
Cinemas, 28, 122, 124
Clervaux, 167
Climate, 10
Clubs: Amateur dramatics, 113, 120, 123
  General, 112–19, 120, 123, 183
  International, 111, 119, 123
  Sports', 114–15, 123
  Women's, 108–11, 119, 122–3, 192, 195
Communion, solemn, 29
Concerts, 121, 124
Council services, 74, 84
Courtrai (Kortrijk), 155–6
Crystal, 178
Cuisine, 10, 25–7, 125–8, 138
Culture, 10
Culture shock, 20, 177

198

Index

Currency, 9
Customs office, 180

Delicatessens, 132
Dentists, 14, 23, 105–6
Diamonds, 179
Dinant, 161
Doctors, 14, 23, 102–3
Driving, 23, 184
 Parking, 147–8
 Rules of the Road, 144–7
 Speed limit, 148
Durbuy, 162

Ecaussinnes-Lalaing, 164
Echternach, 124, 166, 168
Economy: Belgium's, 21, 39–40
 Luxembourg's, 48
Ehnen, 168
Electricity, 69–71, 79, 83, 177, 193, 194
Embassy, 16, 19, 178, 184, 193
Employment, 32, 47, 183
Esch-sur-Sûre, 166
Estate agents, 58–9
Etiquette, 25
Exchange rate, 9, 42
Executive search agencies, 33
Exhibitions, art, 122, 124, 153

Family allowance, 38
Ferries, 169, 170
Festivals: Beer, 164
 Music, 121, 124
 Theatre, 124, 167
Firebacks, 179
Fish, 126–7
Folklore, 10
Food, Ethnic, 133
Foy-Notre-Dame, 163
Francorchamps, 162
Funerals, 29, 30–1
Furnishings, soft, 77, 84

Furniture, 75–7, 84

Game, 127, 131–2, 168
Gas, 69–71, 79, 83, 177, 194
 Butane, 71
 Natural, 71
 Propane, 71
Ghent (Gent), 156–7
Good conduct and morality, certificate of, 15, 80, 84
Grocer's, 132–3
Gynaecologists, 105

Hainaut, 163
Hairdresser, 28
Health service, 101–7
Help line, 21, 116
Help service, 21, 96, 116, 185, 195
Holiday money, 35
Holidays: paid, 36–7
 public, 36
Hospitals, 104–5, 107
Hotels, 19, 164
Household appliances, 17, 77, 84
Hovercraft, 169, 170
Huy, 161

Identity card, 15, 18, 79–80, 84
Import duties and licences, 17
Income tax, 36, 43–7, 51, 178
 Declaration, 45–6, 51
 Payments, 46
Industry: Belgium's, 39
 Luxembourg's, 48
Insenborn, 166
Insurance: Car, 141–2
 Family liability, 79
 Household, 78
 Medical, 101–2
 Work Accident, 78–9

Jetfoil, 169, 170
Jewellery, 179

Jumet, 164

Kalmthoutse Heide, 158
Knokke-Le Zoute, 154
Koksijde, 154

Lace, 178
Language, 7, 9, 21–3, 31, 54
Language courses, 98, 189–190
Lease, 60–1, 62, 65, 69, 177, 179
Libraries, 119, 123, 185
Licences, 80–3, 194
 Antique firearms, 83, 184–5
 Bicycle, 81
 Dog, 82
 Driving, 15, 80–1, 84, 193
 Fishing, 83, 85, 173, 193
 Gun, 83, 184–5
 Hunting, 82–3, 85, 189, 194
 Radio, 82, 85, 186
 Television, 82, 85, 186
Liège, 9, 161–2, 169, 179
Lifestyle, 24
Light fittings, 17, 78
Linen, 178
Liquers, 138
Lochristi, 157
Luxembourg city, 9, 165–6, 174, 179

Mardasson Memorial, 163
Markets, 137–8, 166
Mechelse Heide, 158
Medical treatment, 16
Metro, 149–150
Molenheide, 159
Mons, 153, 170
Montdorf-les-Bains, 168
Moselle, 167, 168
Motoring organisations, 148–9, 194

199

Index

Motorways, 148, 170
Museums, 122, 153, 155, 158, 159, 165, 167

Namur, 161
Newspapers, 33, 47, 174, 175, 185–6

Oostduinkerke, 154
Opera, 120, 124
Ostend (Oostende), 153–4, 169, 170
Overijse, 128, 164

Paediatric clinics, 105
Pageants, 163
Passport, 15, 18, 80
Pewter, 178
Planckendael, 158
Porcelain, 179
Post, 171, 174
Poultry, 132
Processions, 166
Professional card, 16, 186
Property, 52–66
  Letting in Britain, 11–13
  To buy in Belgium/Luxembourg, 63–4
Puppets, 121, 179

Radio, 77, 124, 173, 175
Registration, 79–80, 84, 192
Remich, 167
Removal companies, 17, 177
Residence permit, temporary, 15
Restaurants, 26, 27, 125–8
Ronquières, 160
Royalty, Grand Duchess, 8
  King Baudouin of the Belgians, 8
  Queen Victoria, 10

St Hubert, 163
St-Martens-Latem, 157
Salaries, 35–6

Schengen, 168
Scheuerberg, 167
Schools, 8, 14, 54, 86–96, 176–7, 187–9
  American, 90, 187, 188, 194
  Art, 98, 185
  Ballet, 98, 185
  Belgian, 90, 91–6, 189
  Dance, 98, 185
  English-speaking, 14, 88–9, 90–1, 187–8
  European, 89–90, 99, 187, 188, 194
  In Luxembourg, 19, 99–100
  Kindergarten, 86–8, 187–8
  Other, 91, 188
  Playgroups, 87–8, 187–8
  Primary, 86–9, 187–8
  Secondary, 86–7, 89–91, 187–8
Secretarial agencies, 33
Shops, 28, 53
  Clothes, 137
  Department stores, 137
  Discount, 134
  Do-it-Yourself, 137
  'Drug stores', 134
  Hypermarkets, 134
  Ironmongers, 134–7
  Self-service, 133
  Shoes, 137
  Supermarkets, 133–4, 139
Sickness funds, 101
Size, 9
Social security, 36, 38–9, 47, 189
Souvenirs, 178
Spa, 162
Sports, Canoeing, 162–3, 167
  Roller-skating, 168
  Sailing, 167
Sports equipment, 179

Stock exchange, 43
Survey, 61

Taxi, 27, 150, 152
Telephone, 72–4, 79, 83–4, 177, 190, 194
Telephone books, 74, 84
Television, 77–8, 122, 124, 173, 175
Temping agencies, 34
Tipping, 27, 28
Tourist offices, 165, 168, 190–1, 195
Tournai, 164
Train, 150–1, 152, 169
Tram, 149

University, 8, 96–8, 98–9, 100, 191–2

Value Added Tax (VAT/TVA/BTW), 17, 40, 48, 84, 139
Veurne, 156
Vianden, 167
Visa, 16, 19, 80

Wallonia, 10
Wasserbillig, 168
Water, 69–71, 79, 83, 177, 192, 194
Waterloo, 160
Weddings, 29–30
Wellenstein, 167
Wieze, 164
Wills, 18, 47
Wiltz, 167
Wine, 27, 138, 167
Work contract, 19, 34–5
Work permit, 15, 34, 47, 79–80
Working hours, 35, 37, 47
World War I, 48, 156
World War II, 10

Ypres (Ieper), 156

Zeebrugge, 170
Zolder, 159
Zoutleeuw, 176
Zwin, 154